The Story of King Lo

ลิลิตพระลอ

The Story of King Lo
Lilit Phra Lo

Translated by

Robert J. Bickner

Silkworm Books

ลิลิตพระลอ
ISBN: 978-616-215-160-6
© 2020 Silkworm Books

First published in 2020 by
Silkworm Books
430/58 M. 7, T. Mae Hia, Chiang Mai 50100, Thailand
info@silkwormbooks.com
http://www.silkwormbooks.com

Typeset in Minion Pro 11 pt. by Silk Type
Printed and bound in Thailand by O. S. Printing House, Bangkok

5 4 3 2 1

For my wife, Patcharin,
the greatest gift that life has given me.

CONTENTS

FOREWORD

I first came to know of the poem *Lilit Phra Lo* during my days in graduate school at the University of Michigan. Professor William J. Gedney, seeing that he had a half dozen or so students of Thai who were interested in the literature of the language, offered to organize a seminar class on Thai poetry. The first piece we looked at was *Lilit Phra Lo*, and the fascination I discovered for the text has been with me ever since. I eventually decided to make it the subject of my PhD dissertation, and then of a subsequent monograph. Through all the years of my teaching and administrative work at the University of Wisconsin I tinkered with one aspect of the text or another, and here, at long last, is my complete translation. I don't know exactly why it took so very long to finish—in truth, I completed the bulk of the translation many years ago. But it always seemed a great challenge to bring together all of the many thoughts and impressions that surround the text in my imagination. Today, I still have a hard time convincing myself that the task is complete, but now is finally the time to share this focus of my work with others.

Many friends and colleagues have helped me as I've pursued my interest in the text, so many that I despair of being able to include all those to whom I am indebted. I hope that those who recall discussing the text with me over the years will indulge me once more by accepting my thanks to all at once.

In the end, though, there are a few people I must thank individually. One is Dr. Chris Baker, who has read my drafts and has provided me with numerous helpful suggestions. I am greatly indebted to him, and to Dr. Phasuk Phongpaichit, for all their help and encouragement, as well as the subtle, and very helpful, prodding to get it done.

Finally, I must offer my profound thanks to my wife, Patcharin Peyasantiwong. She has been with me, supporting and caring about me, ever since we met. She was there at the beginning of this project and never gave up on me, even at those times when I came close to giving up on myself. There simply are no words to express how important she is to me, how grateful I am to her for all she has given me, or how very deeply I love her.

Robert J. Bickner
Verona, Wisconsin
July 2019

INTRODUCTION

"The Story of King Lo," known in Thai as *Lilit Phra Lo* was assigned a place in the Thai canon by the Literary Association (*Wannakhadi samoson*), a body brought into being in 1914 by decree of King Vajiravudh (Rama VI, r. 1910–25). With that royal acclamation, the story has ever since been included in a group of texts deemed worthy of the then newly created designation *wannakhadi*, which was coined to be the equivalent of the Western concept of "literature." The story, still held in high regard today, is included in every listing of significant Thai literary texts and is a part of school and university curricula throughout the country. At least one stanza from it has dutifully been consigned to memory by countless numbers of Thai schoolchildren, and the poem's verse forms, although now archaic and difficult to use, still appear. Portions of the story have been enacted in costumed dance, and an English-language adaptation, *The Magic Lotus*, was once broadcast by the BBC.

Scholars have invested much time and effort in describing the text and interpreting the meaning of *Lilit Phra Lo*'s sometimes obscure passages. Over the years various reasons have been put forth to justify the story's membership in the canon and to explain its ongoing esteem. It has been lauded as beautiful poetry, as an evocation of deep emotion, and as a depiction of kingly virtues. It has been praised both as a beautiful representation of rural culture and as a window into bygone court life. It has been referred to as Buddhist literature, suggesting that it exemplifies Buddhist values and practices. And many Thai scholars and teachers have engaged in prolonged studies and disputations about when the tale came into being and who should be credited with its creation.

Upon close examination, however, each of the suggested reasons for the admiration of the tale seems weak in one way or another. The poetry of the text is beautiful but not as ornate or melodic to the modern ear as is poetry in forms of the present day. Also, it has been criticized (politely) for assumed poetic lapses—anomalous spellings, for example, are numerous, as are passages with apparently incorrect syllable counts. Modern critics have also noted suspected forced rhymes and seeming irregularity in tone positioning, which appears to have been a structural component of the ancient forms. These and other apparent flaws in the text are explained as purposeful distortions created by ancient poets who lacked the skill and discipline of their better-educated modern counterparts, who would not tolerate such weaknesses in their own work.[1] The single deep emotion that is depicted in the story is grief, and the single quality that might be considered kingly virtue could also be seen as mere bravado in the face of certain death. Not mentioned in the praise for the poem is that the main character is a king who abandons his family and his kingdom to pursue by stealth a sexual liaison in the palace of a rival. Rural culture of the time is hardly more than referred to, and then only briefly and in passing. Court life appears in only slightly more detail. References to Buddhist values and practices are, at best, difficult to discern, while far more obvious are references to Hindu ceremonies and divinities, and to spells and magic not comfortably associated with the Theravada Buddhism of modern Thailand. Quite apart from any other aspect of the tale, it has also been criticized—and on this point not at all politely—as a vulgar piece of ancient titillation,[2] worthy only of being consigned to the flames.

Thus, those who seek to understand *Lilit Phra Lo* and take the full measure of its significance in the literary and cultural history of Thailand must grapple with daunting puzzles, foremost among them the greatly divergent views of the text. Is it, on the one hand, a worthy member of the royally created canon,[3] fit for on-going scholarly acclaim? Or is it, on the other hand, a notably flawed work by inferior poets who created erotica for ancient elites? In either case, the story is little known outside of Thailand; even for academic specialists, the story remains largely unstudied and inaccessible. Many native speakers of Thai who admire the text also readily admit that they find significant portions difficult to follow, and even those who have studied the text extensively disagree about how to interpret many passages. Archaic vocabulary, now-unfamiliar phrasing, and passages that seem out of step with poetic norms can leave the modern reader at a loss.

The many puzzling aspects of the story—such as questions about its origins, authorship, and purpose—do not allow for easy solutions. These questions have been the focus of modern studies of the text but still await satisfying answers. Those answers often seem to lie just beyond the grasp of the modern reader, in roughly the same way that real appreciation of Shakespeare or of Chaucer's *The Canterbury Tales* seems close enough to invite interest, but appreciation ultimately lies tantalizingly out of reach without specialized background. Close study of those texts has helped modern students of English literature come to appreciate them more fully, just as *Lilit Phra Lo* will similarly come to be appreciated more fully but only with further detailed study.

Despite all the difficulties, or perhaps because of them, studying *Lilit Phra Lo* is a fascinating challenge. In it are the elements of an engaging story, complete with powerful kings leading magnificent armies, mysterious sorcerers commanding terrifying powers, and youthful infatuation tragically thwarted by vengeful elders. Looking deeper into the story is more difficult. The difficulties that can obscure the tale involve two crucial factors that have not yet been fully taken into account: language change over time, and change in the nature and purpose of storytelling.

Lilit Phra Lo is arguably the oldest Thai narrative that can be attributed to the time when ancient speech patterns were still in place, and so it is well worth close study, no matter how many obstacles stand in our path. The challenges are complex, but they are surely part of why this story remains fascinating even many centuries after it was first told.

Sources for *Lilit Phra Lo*

The full text of the tale has been printed and reprinted many times, most consistently in a low-cost edition published by the Thai Ministry of Education, intended for use in the nation's schools. This edition is bound in simple paper covers, without illustrations, commentary, or interpretation, though it does include a glossary consisting primarily of words that by modern judgments are spelled problematically. Footnotes give simple translations for some obscure vocabulary, and some alternate readings that appear in older, unpublished manuscript volumes but without comment or elaboration. This presentation also introduces an important innovation: straightforward sequential numbering of all stanzas of the text, making this the only edition that is practical to use as the basis for detailed comparison and study, and it is followed in this translation.

Over the years, private printing houses have also produced their own editions that are intended for a general audience. Such editions usually confine themselves to the text, but cover illustrations, perhaps reflecting prevailing attitudes of the time, differ in interesting ways. Some depict simple views of rural life, others the formality of royal courts, others what seems to be only lightly veiled licentiousness. Despite what the very different cover treatments might suggest, though, the text is virtually identical in each of these editions.

The most comprehensive treatment of the story is that of Chanthit Krasaesin. His *Prachum wannakhadi Thai: Phak 2 Phra Lo Lilit* (Thai literature collection: Part 2 Lilit Phra Lo), the product of many years of work, finally saw publication in 1954. Although its availability is more limited than that of other sources, the study can be found in some research libraries with extensive Thai-language collections. The book includes a lengthy introduction with a complete text and stanza-by-stanza interpretation and, in a significant departure from all other sources, also includes both a main reading and compilations of variant readings for many stanzas, taken from among the versions of the story that the author was able to locate.[4] Ultimately, he viewed nearly all the variations as erroneous or inferior to the published wording and did not see the significance of the variations that he found. He also devised his own numbering system for the poem, but it is internally inconsistent and so complicates rather than enhances any effort to use his work for comparative study.

Companion books are often used to introduce Thai readers to complex subjects and texts of many types, and probably the most visible one for the Phra Lo story is that of Phra Worawetphisit, widely known as Phra Worawet, a long-time instructor of Thai literature at

Chulalongkorn University in Bangkok. His *Khu mue Lilit Phra Lo* (Handbook for Lilit Phra Lo) has appeared in print in two formats, both as a single volume and at least once in two volumes. Some of these editions have shown interesting but unacknowledged internal variations, from 1961 though 1987; these editions can also be found in the collections of some research libraries. The author includes definitions for individual vocabulary items and phrases, a lengthy glossary, and rephrasing for each stanza. Unfortunately, he uses an idiosyncratic numbering system that frustrates attempts at cross-referencing, and he omits any consideration of manuscript variations.

The most recent of such efforts, *An Lilit Phra Lo: Chabap wikhro lae thot khwam* (Reading Lilit Phra Lo: Analysis and interpretation), by Professor Cholada Ruengruglikit of Silpakorn University, includes a full text with rephrasings and definitions of problem vocabulary following each stanza. This treatment goes well beyond any predecessor, however, by including descriptive and insightful analytical treatments of the text's prosody, themes, and motifs.

All of the available sources can be helpful in thinking through the many puzzling aspects of the text, although there are unfortunate limitations. They do not always agree on what passages require clarification, nor do their separate clarifications always agree. Also, they do not attempt to account for the significant variations that can be found in the extant manuscript volumes now held in the collection of the National Library of Thailand. Phra Worawet, for example, hardly acknowledges the variations in the manuscript volumes at all. And while Chanthit takes pains to compile variant readings from manuscript volumes, there are many others that he does not include; it may be that volumes were added to the library collection after he had completed his compilation. More tellingly though, his stated preferences for one wording over others are nearly always based on modern poetic tastes and so are often historically inaccurate.[5]

Other versions of the story have appeared at various times. A few summaries and précis can be found in library collections, but they are not intended to substitute for the text itself. Pluang Na Nakhorn, for one, includes a lengthy excerpt in his *Prawat wannakhadi Thai* (History of Thai literature),[6] in which he makes no mention of the source for the excerpt and does not address manuscript variations. A spoken drama based on the poem "The Magic Lotus," by Prem Chaya, was well received—it was once broadcast by the BBC—and was available for a time in print. Each of these versions is interesting in its own way, but they do not take the place of the full text.

Most Thai resources for study of the story were completed prior to the development of modern linguistics. Comparative and historical studies of Thai did not become widely recognized and available until after pre-modern Thai scholars had completed their work. The great gulf between the older and established field of literary studies, on the one hand, and the newer and still less-esteemed field of linguistics, on the other, has been bridged only partly. While that separation may not have a significant impact on studies of more modern texts, it remains a significant limitation for studies of *Lilit Phra Lo*. Approaching the text from the perspective of literary studies alone omits the fact that it came into existence at a time when Thai speech was significantly different. Without the linguistic facts as context, modern tastes and preferences have often become the basis for evaluations of the text and its verse forms, resulting in unfortunate misunderstandings.

Locating the Story

Popular belief asserts that the tale originated in the northern part of present-day Thailand. Folklore has it that a stupa located in modern Phrae Province, and by some accounts approximately four hundred years old, is the resting place of the remains of Phra Lo and the two princesses, Phra Phuean and Phra Phaeng. Convincing evidence for such contentions has not yet been brought forward. Some scholars think the language of the text demonstrates a northern origin, and along with vocabulary point to the use of the negative particle, *bo* (not), which appears in some modern dialects spoken in areas of northern and northeastern Thailand, and in Laos. Cholada characterizes approximately two dozen words as archaic or northern Thai vocabulary, as well as approximately a dozen words of Khmer origin.[7] M. R. Sumonnachat Sawatdikun, in his extensive and broadly based treatment of the text *Sop suan rueang kan taeng Phra Lo* (Investigation into the composition of Phra Lo), first published in 1945, points to the use of the now archaic dual pronoun system, noting that system's use during the Sukhothai period, although he does not specify whether he believes the text came from this time or later, during the Ayutthaya period.[8] While each of these observations is intriguing, more analysis is needed before firm conclusions can be drawn; for one thing, the text has surely changed considerably over time, and knowing how consistent the variations are throughout its entirety may help to isolate older sections from more recent insertions.

Sumonnachat makes a notable attempt to locate the events of the story in real space, mainly by looking for geographical features in the region that seem to match the content of the text. While his considerations are lengthy and detailed, there is in fact, very little specific information in *Lilit Phra Lo* to go on. We are told at the end of stanza five, and again in stanza six, for example, that the territory under the control of the city of Suang lies to the west, and that of Song to the east, although on that point not all of the manuscript volumes agree, with a few reversing that. Also, that assertion in stanza five seems oddly out of context with the rest of the content of the stanza, as though it had been inserted as an afterthought. The text describes the two ladies-in-waiting as passing through a forest and ascending a mountain when they go to meet the sorcerer Samingphrai. Later, when Phra Lo travels in search of Phra Phuean and Phra Phaeng, he must cross a river named "Kalong" (at an unspecified crossing place). No other such details appear in the text, despite the lengthy journeys.

Only a very few details of the story, then, seem even vaguely reminiscent of actual topography, and it is most unlikely that they were ever intended as references to specific locations. In any case, attempts to locate the story in real space hold out little hope of telling us anything of significance; the substance of the text belongs more comfortably in the realm of myth and imagination than in the realm of historical fact.

Dating the Text

Determining the age and authorship of *Lilit Phra Lo* has long been a significant concern in Thai academic circles and Thai textbooks.[9] The story does not concern itself with historical figures or events that might provide specific reference points, so many attempts at dating have been based largely on impressionistic comparison with other texts. Some attempts have focused on specific details presumed to place the text's roots in a particular historical period.

The "king" vs. "prince" controversy

Much speculation, as well as sometimes heated debate, has been based on a contrast between the wording found in the final two stanzas (659 and 660) of the poem in the edition of the Ministry of Education. The wording seems to associate the text with specific yet unnamed personalities. The first of the stanzas attributes the creation of the story to a "great king," and the second attributes its rendering in written form to a "noble prince." A great deal of scholarly effort has been devoted to trying to determine which period in Thai history can provide an appropriate personality to whom to apply the stanzas. Two interpretations have developed. One interpretation sees two individuals: a king who composed the verses, and a prince who dutifully set them down in writing. The second sees a single individual, although it requires convoluted explanations of how that individual, whoever he might have been, managed to compose the text while ruling as a king, and also set it down while a prince. Whichever interpretation a given scholar favors, the approach has been to comb through the various accounts of all the periods of Thai history, looking to link the text to a specific historical figure or figures.

In considering the content of these two stanzas it is helpful to recall that the tale as we know it today does not begin until the fifth stanza and that it ends with stanza 658. The stanzas that appear prior to the action of the tale are words of tribute to an unnamed ruler of the city of Ayutthaya, and those that come afterward speak of an unnamed royal author or scribe. I have argued elsewhere[10] that both structural and thematic considerations demonstrate the very strong likelihood that all six of these stanzas were added to the text after it had already come into common use, casting doubt from the outset on the usefulness of the argument over authorship. However, so much attention has been devoted to an assumed contrast between the final two stanzas that it is still important to look very closely at the controversy they have engendered. And it is in the manuscript volumes of the text, rather than the printed editions, that we find the crucial detail that eliminates the grounds for dispute.

Of the thirteen manuscripts that contain stanza 659, all have a term that means "king": ten copies have the term *maharat* that we see in the printed editions, while three copies have the still respectful but somewhat less laudatory *phrarat*. The stanza that is numbered 660— that is, the final stanza of the published versions, appears in only twelve manuscript volumes, but all of them have the term *maharat* instead of the word *yaowarat* (prince) that we see in printed editions. The reading found in this final stanza in the printed texts, therefore, dates only to the time of the introduction of print technology to Thailand. All the complex speculation based on a supposed contrast between these stanzas is really based only on a modern insertion into the text, a modern corruption, in fact. The argument has no historical foundation.

Curiously, the Ministry of Education text (p. 162) has a footnote for the stanza giving the uncorrupted wording but stating inaccurately that it is to be found in only two manuscript volumes. The Ministry of Fine Arts edition, on the other hand, acknowledges the error in its brief introduction but then preserves that error in the text, saying that it would be preferable to refrain from making any changes to the wording until all could be done at once. Chanthit (xcix–cx; 738–39) notes the spurious wording and acknowledges that it appeared initially only in the first printed edition of the poem (which he dates to 1875 or possibly 1869) and states clearly that it is not to be found in any manuscript copies. While Chanthit acknowledges the confusion that the insertion of *yaowarat* has led to, however, he still preserves the error as his main reading. The unfortunate result of the editorial decisions made for each of these presentations of the story is that they perpetuate an acknowledged error, giving credence to the useless speculation that it engenders.

It is interesting to note also that manuscript volume 35 in the National Library includes stanza 659 but not stanza 660; there is unused space on that page in which an additional stanza could easily have been written, so it does not appear that any material has been accidently omitted or lost, suggesting the possibility that volume 35 was completed before stanza 660 was added to the text. If so, that stanza might not predate the middle of the nineteenth century when the extant manuscripts were created—centuries after the tale came into being, and long after it was replaced in popular use by stories in modern *klon* poetic forms.

This effort to establish the date and authorship of the tale fails to lead to a satisfying conclusion, and its failure serves to spotlight a larger problem. First, the texts must be as accurate as possible in all their details. It is ineffective to draw conclusions about the age of the story based on a wording change that was made as recently as 150 or so years ago. Changes that were made long before print technology came into being must also be taken into account. The four introductory stanzas and the two concluding ones all serve the purposes of a monarchical state that sees value in asserting its power and preeminence. By theme and structure these six stanzas differ so much from the story of King Lo that they must have been added after the fact and so must not be considered when attempting to determine either age or authorship—and yet that is what has been done.

What's in a Name?

The spelling of the name of the great historical capital Ayutthaya has also been a point of speculation. While that focus may seem appropriate at first glance, the same two important problems must be addressed. First, the name of the city appears only in the first and second stanzas of the poem as we know it today, in the portion of the text that is thematically and structurally separate from the tale itself. It is quite likely to have been added to the story at some time after it first came into being, and there is no way to know just how long the interval might have been. Second, along with focusing on a portion of the text that is likely to be more recent than the tale itself, this attempt considers only the printed versions of the poem. Examination of the manuscript volumes demonstrates clearly why speculation based only on currently available printed versions cannot be successful. For the word in question here, two different spellings appear in the manuscript versions of the first stanza: "Ayutthaya" and "Ayotthaya"; of the nineteen extant volumes that include this stanza, a total of thirteen have the former spelling, while five have the latter spelling, and one is illegible at this point. Even if it were possible to draw a conclusion based on the spelling of a single word that appears only twice in a text that has clearly been altered considerably over centuries, it is not possible to determine a date when the entire tale came into being based on such narrow and conflicting considerations.

External Chronologies

Over and above the focus on the spelling of "Ayutthaya," the material found in the first stanza of the tale as it currently exists is also cited as evidence for its age, and this in reference to the dynastic struggles of that period. The capital, and by extension its ruler, is acclaimed for having attained mastery over the Lao Kao, the Yuan, and the Lao, all closely related rivals for power. Periods at which it is known that Ayutthaya was at war with those rivals are then cited as the likely point of origin for the story. Such conflicts, however, are not mentioned anywhere else in the text. The story of Phra Lo exists quite independently of any such rivalries, and no ethnic terms appear anywhere else in the story. The problem is again that the tale more than likely predates the beginning stanzas, which were almost certainly added to satisfy subsequent dynastic concerns.

Speculation about the age of the tale has also attempted to incorporate the local history of technological innovation. In stanza 8, and again in 229, the reader encounters the term *puen fai*, a compound of *puen* which refers to a weapon for hurling projectiles, and *fai*, or "fire."[11] It has been suggested that the term as it is used here refers to cannon and so the poem must date from after the arrival of such weapons. At first glance this idea seems reasonable.

The difficulty, though, is in trying to establish the meaning of the term *puen* at any given point in history. In modern usage, it generally equates with the English "gun," but as the Dictionary of the Royal Institute in 1999 (p. 701) suggests, the term has evolved to encompass a number of different technologies beginning with the crossbow, a term that also appears in stanza 8. Chanthit (23–24) believes that the reference is to the flintlock rifle, which, like the cannon that would come only later, would have been terrifyingly loud and lethal to those not familiar with the technology. Joaquim De Campos in his article "Early Portuguese Accounts of Thailand" (p. 8–9) points to the passage of many years between the arrival of gunpowder in the area and the time at which it was adopted for warfare, which means that we have a potentially long period of time in which both the technology and the terms used to refer to it would have been in flux. In a discussion of the use of the term in the Palatine Law

(*Kot monthianban*) of about 1450, he speculates that the term might at that time have been used to refer to "flame throwers such as the mangonels which were also used to throw inflammable materials." So, we have both developing technology and developing terminology and the combination does not offer much in the way of precision. Since oral texts change over time we cannot be sure when a specific detail was first included, and in this case, we cannot be sure exactly what the term meant to speakers of any specific era.

In considering age and authorship of the text, we will probably never be able to arrive at any certainty. We must also accept that looking at isolated points, whether specific words, phrasing patterns, or any of the other details that have been cited as evidence, will not give satisfying results because they cannot reliably be applied throughout the text, leaving too much uncertainty to be helpful.

If, on the other hand, we begin with more general questions and establish a context in which to examine the text in its entirety, then we can proceed on a more solid footing. We should begin with what we now know of language change over time, and what we can say of the differences between modern Thai and its ancient predecessor, the speech in which the story originated. We must also consider what ideas about the nature of a text and about storytelling must have been like in the oral culture of centuries long past, and consider how they would have differed from ideas of the print-oriented culture of today. We will then be ready to look comprehensively at the text and the poetic forms that appear in it. Doing so will also allow us to clarify issues about *Lilit Phra Lo* that have troubled modern scholars, to put to rest doubts about the skills of ancient poets, and to appreciate their abilities all the more deeply.

Thai Language at the Time of *Lilit Phra Lo*

One point about which native speakers of Thai will all agree is that the language of *Lilit Phra Lo* "feels old," despite being unable to quantify that reaction, just as native speakers of English can agree that the language of Shakespeare, or Chaucer, who wrote the older and quite obscure *The Canterbury Tales*, feels old without being able to pinpoint details to explain that reaction. In general, speakers of both languages would be able to agree that the language of the texts in question seems familiar in some ways but not in others, and that some of it is easily understood while some cannot be fathomed, and in any case, it is clearly not the speech of the present day.

In the case of *The Canterbury Tales*, we know that much of the difference is the result of what is known as the Great Vowel Shift, an array of systemic changes in the phonology of the language, seen most clearly in the vowel system, that took place after Chaucer's work was completed. Although that text can be very difficult to understand without study, we can still read and even appreciate the written representation of some of that poetry. But we also know that if we were to read it aloud, our rendering would sound quite different from what it would have sounded like when it came into being.

In the case of *Lilit Phra Lo*, a comparable difference exists between the speech of the time it came into being and contemporary Thai speech. As with English, an array of systemic phonological changes took place; the most obvious change occurred in the vowel system and has been dubbed the Great Tone Shift.[12] Those changes took place at some point after *Lilit Phra Lo* came into being.

The aspect of these changes that is most crucial for understanding *Lilit Phra Lo* is the transformation of what we now know as "tone." Ancient poetic forms, unlike those of more recent times, made structural use of the ancient tone categories as they existed prior to the Great Tone Shift: three contrastive tones for syllables that ended in a sonorant sound, as opposed to the modern five found in the majority of Thai dialects. Many other aspects of the phonological system also changed over time, but the shift from three tones to five is the most consequential of them for study of the story of Phra Lo, because that change in the tone system seems also to have altered one of the building blocks of ancient poetry—the nature and function of rhyme.

In ancient Thai speech, rhyme included a match of one of the three ancient tone categories, which are known today as "common" or "ordinary" (*saman*), "first" (*ek*), and "second" (*tho*).[13] Orthographically, words of the common category were not marked, but words of the first and second categories were written with the first and second markers, respectively. For lack of a better term, we refer to these three categories as "tone," though we do not know what features actually characterized the three categories in ancient speech.[14]

For the study of *Lilit Phra Lo*, it is not crucial to speculate about what ancient pronunciations sounded like; what is important, however, is that in the ancient system a given word could have rhymed only with another word from within the same tone category, that is "common" category words could have rhymed only with other "common" category words, and so on.[15] In the modern system, on the other hand, the ancient tone categories are no longer acoustically distinct; that is, the same tone contours can be found in more than one ancient category, and so tone has ceased to be an integral part of rhyme. In the ancient system, two words rhymed if they were from the same tone category and had both the same vowel and final consonant sound, if any. In the modern system, tone is removed from that definition, and a match between vowel and any final consonant sound is sufficient to create a valid rhyme. With tone category removed from the concept of rhyme, the possibilities for creating rhyme were vastly increased, and the status of rhyme changed from a defining feature of auditory structure to a decorative role, as we see in modern poetic forms.

Implicit in modern work on *Lilit Phra Lo* is the unspoken assumption that the language of the ancient poets was essentially the same as that of the present day. Familiar with modern *klon* poetry, in which rhyme has proliferated, most notably with the work of the poetic genius Sunthon Phu, who exploited the possibilities of rhyme to the greatest extent possible,[16] modern scholars have unwittingly judged the text of *Lilit Phra Lo* by measures of what would satisfy modern tastes, and using techniques ultimately based on poetic texts of Indic origin. The negative judgments that many scholars have made, and the supposed weaknesses they have identified, are based on misconceptions about ancient speech and poetry. The ancient poets, rather than being inferior to those of the present day, were every bit as adept, creative, and masterful, but they spoke a language that was significantly different from that of the present day and were working in an oral medium rather than a written one.

The unrecognized difference between ancient speech and modern speech is at the basis of much modern criticism of the text and has engendered the spurious idea that ancient poets, in order to satisfy the rhyme placement conventions, purposely violated spelling norms and created what came to be labeled *thot* (erroneous) or *bangkhap* (required) spellings.[17] A number of such words appear in the text, enough to give credence to the negative evaluation of the ancient poets and their work. Once accepted, the idea that the ancient poets resorted to such distortions expanded to explain away nearly everything in the texts that seemed problematic. Rather than being evidence of poetic ineptitude, however, the anomalies are evidence of language change over time. The negative evaluation, in all its variations, is baseless. Ancient poets were not less accomplished than modern ones, but they were working in a language that was fundamentally different from that of today.[18]

The change in the tone system, and the consequent change in the nature of rhyme, may help to explain other anomalies in the text as well, such as the difference in word order in expressions that appear in the text and that are still used in modern speech. A striking example is the expression *phaephai*.[19] Modern users recognize the two components of the expression but note that they appear in reverse order of the modern pattern, which is *phaiphae* (to lose). In the ancient text, however, both the word order and the meaning are reversed, with *phaephai* clearly meaning "to win." The word *phai* is glossed in the Royal Institute Dictionary (p. 784) as a verb meaning "to flee" or "to lose." And while the word *phae* in modern Thai means "to lose," in all other dialects of the language family it means the opposite—"to win." Modern Thai is thus alone in reversing the meaning of the word, and the 1999 Royal Institute Dictionary entry (p. 803) is mistaken in listing "to lose" as a secondary and archaic meaning.

Considering how this particular change must have come about gives a hint to the age of the text and the significance of the change in the nature of rhyme. The older phrase, the one that appears in the poem, must originally have been a compound of two verbs, *phae* "to win" and *phai* "to flee," with the resulting phrase perhaps meaning something like "to conquer and [to cause] to flee." The meaning reversal, in which "to win" came to mean "to lose," may be the result of a misinterpretation of the more recent wording preference of *phaiphae*, which originally would have been another phrase, this one perhaps meaning "to flee [before] the victors." Later speakers evidently came to think of the phrase not as a compound of two distinct words but as a doublet, a very common feature of modern speech, in which two phonetically similar words have parallel or related meanings, in this case inviting an interpretation something like "to flee and [therefore] lose." Doublets, known in Thai as *khamsoi*, are very common in modern speech and poetic texts in *klon* forms,[20] but they are not found in the Phra Lo story. One must wonder, in fact, if the doublet, or any aspect of the larger phenomenon known as reduplication, featured at all in speech prior to the development of the modern five-tone system, which with its vastly increased possibilities for creating rhyme made reduplication a possibility.[21] In this respect, too, the language of the text suggests that it came to be when the language was fundamentally different. As I argue elsewhere, the invocation before the beginning of the Phra Lo story was added after the story came into being, but it is still very old; its sentiment if not its content is much in keeping with a time when Ayutthaya was in competition with nearby kingdoms for dominance, but it does not seem to be in keeping with the nature of the Phra Lo story itself.[22]

One mostly unexplored linguistic aspect suggestive of the text's age is the now archaic and largely forgotten dual pronoun system used throughout the story. The three forms in the paradigm are the first-person dual pronoun *phuea* (we two), the second-person dual pronoun *khuea* (you two), and the third-person dual pronoun *kha* (they two)."[23] The manuscript volumes are inconsistent in using all three of the pronouns, suggesting that they were already a source of confusion at the time that the extant copies were being made, most likely in the mid-1800s or later. It comes as no surprise then that printed editions, and explications and précis of the text, are similarly confused. Those who study the text for insight into the society from which it developed, especially with respect to concepts of status, should note this problem.

The Poetic Forms of *Lilit Phra Lo*

The basic unit of the ancient poetic form in which *Lilit Phra Lo* is told is a hemistich, or *wak*, of five stressed syllables, subdivided into two phrases of unequal length—almost always a two-syllable grouping and a three-syllable one, in either order. Each hemistich is also almost always a complete syntactic unit and is further embellished in one of two ways to create a stanza type. One such embellishment is a rhyme link between the last syllable of one hemistich and a syllable within the first phrase of the next, resulting in a chain of consecutively linked hemistichs of indeterminate number, some rather short with as few as four and others quite long, with several hundred hemistichs. The rhythm of such linked hemistichs in recitation would likely have remained consistent throughout the stanza. A stanza made up of hemistichs linked in this way is an example of what is known today as *rai* poetry.

The other embellishment, rather than fostering a uniform rhythm, was a separation between hemistichs that in recitation would have interrupted the rhythmic flow. This embellishment is achieved by appending to each full hemistich one that is shorter and has two or four stressed syllables, depending on its position in the stanza. The shorter hemistich creates a rhythmic counterpoint that serves to slow the progression of the recitation. The resulting stanza type is known as *khlong*. The longest type of such stanzas has four full hemistichs, each followed by a shorter one, and is thus known as *khlong si* (*si* means "four"). Stanzas of this type are further embellished with required tone placements throughout the stanza and with two overlapping rhyme patterns, one linking the second, third, and fifth hemistichs and another linking the fourth and seventh hemistichs. The result would have been a stanza that, when recited in the ancient pronunciation system of Thai, must have been one of great acoustic density, with each hemistich distinct from all the others in that stanza.

There is also a third stanza type, one of three hemistichs, that combines elements of both *rai* and *khlong*. It is like *rai* in that it begins with a full hemistich, which is then linked by rhyme to a second full hemistich, although this link is with the final syllable instead of an early one. And it is like *khlong* in that the final two hemistichs are patterned like the final two of a *khlong si* stanza, with the third and final hemistich one of four rather than five syllables. A stanza of this type is called *khlong song* (*song* means "two"), with the name again indicating the number of full hemistichs.[24]

A tale told with a mixture of *rai* and *khlong* stanzas is known as *lilit*—and so the story of Phra Lo is known as *Lilit Phra Lo*.[25]

In performance, all of these elements must have made for an extremely dense auditory pattern. It would have been possible for an attentive member of the audience to have known at any time, and simply by listening, the point in the stanza structure that the recitation had reached, as well as what was still to come in that pattern. At the same time, patterns of rhyme links between stanza types added to the density of the text and indicated to the careful listener the type of stanza that was to follow.[26]

As time went by, the *khlong* and *rai* forms were eventually largely abandoned and replaced by *klon* forms. When the auditory distinctions that had once separated the three ancient tone categories were transformed into modern contour tone, a significant portion of the auditory basis for the old forms was lost. In terms of stanza structure, ambiguity was introduced into the system as the different parts of the ancient system developed identical pitch contours. In the dialects of the central plain of Thailand, some words from the old *ek* category came to have the same contours as some words from the old *tho* category.[27] The ambiguity made it impossible to compose verse in the ancient forms based on sound alone, because distinctions that had been auditory now existed only in orthography, and so both use and appreciation of the forms now required literacy. The poetic forms lost their grounding in the speech of the day. The new forms that replaced them, known as *klon*, became the poetry of their day and have remained so.

Just when Thai speech, and its poetic forms, underwent these changes is not clear. Dialect comparisons do demonstrate clearly that such changes took place in every member of the family, and most likely at about the same time, but more than that is open to speculation. Accounts of foreign visitors are suggestive of when those changes must have been in place. The popular stories mentioned in the accounts of European visitors to the kingdom of Ayutthaya are examples of *klon* poetry, which is based on the modern five-tone system. None of those accounts, on the other hand, most of which were written toward the end of the kingdom's prominence, make mention of *Lilit Phra Lo*, suggesting that the story was no longer performed at the time, no doubt succeeded in popularity by stories told in modern verse.[28] Therefore, we can speculate that the changes took place before the arrival of these European visitors. The number of *klon* works said to have achieved popularity further suggests that the changes must have been in place for some time before their arrival, perhaps since the early Ayutthaya period.

As with all types of poetry indigenous to a given language, *khlong* and *rai* sprang from the normal speech patterns of their time.[29] The ability to create such verse would not have required literacy, since it would have been based on manipulation of sound patterns and not orthographic ones. Thus any member of the speech community, whether lord or subject, merchant or farmer, city dweller or rural peasant, could have appreciated any tale told in these forms. There would not have been any distinction between a court literature and a folk literature, at least not one based on poetic forms or on assumed complexity or sophistication of those forms.[30]

After the older spoken system of three tones developed into a five-tone system, the older sound categories were no longer distinctly separate, and it was no longer possible to rely solely on auditory considerations to create rhyme links that fit the expected placement. Orthography instead came to be crucial, and today composition in these forms requires control of the notably complex Thai spelling system.

Scholarly studies of other traditions can also be instructive. Milman Parry, in his studies of the Homeric tradition of ancient Greek poetry argues that a significant portion of many lines of the *Iliad* and the *Odyssey* were structured to facilitate recitation, so that, for example, fixed phrases such as epithets and elaborate descriptions were frequently employed in contexts for which the exact meanings of the expressions were extraneous. He argues further that storytelling in an oral tradition was not a feat of memory by which a fixed text was recalled exactly, but an act of creativity during which a poet employing formulaic structures created a story anew.[31] With repeated elements serving as standardized building blocks, the difficulty of extemporaneous composition is reduced, and time is provided for the poet to think ahead as the recitation progresses. Repeated elements of this type are not needed for a recitation based on a written text but would have been crucial for an oral presentation based on manipulation of a poetic formula and extemporaneous variation.

Many poetic features of *Lilit Phra Lo* easily lead to conclusions similar to those that Parry reached about Greek poetry. The use of epithets is a clear example. The expression *song si*, consisting of the words "two" and "glory" and meaning something like "the two noble ones," appears thirty-seven times as a reference to the two princesses. The expression *chao la*, "lord of the earth" appears thirty-two times as a reference to Phra Lo, and *song phi liang*, "two attendants," is used eleven times to refer to one or the other of the two pairs of companions, those of the king or those of the princesses. Such repetition would not be deemed appropriate in a modern composition, and it must have served some purpose in the ancient texts. If we accept Parry's contention that for ancient Greek poetry the purpose of such repeated expressions is to facilitate the telling of long and complex stories that are familiar to both poet and audience but that also varied in each presentation, then we have an explanation that fits the Thai case equally well and that suggests we should view the story of Phra Lo as originating in an oral culture.

If there are elements of storytelling that appear in both ancient Greek and ancient Thai tales, there are also characteristics of Thai poetry that do not appear in Greek, but to which Parry's insights seem to apply nonetheless. Rhyme, for example, functions in each *rai* or *khlong* stanza as a structural rather than decorative element. In other words, there could have been no counterpart to the modern distinction between rhyme within a poetic unit, or internal rhyme (*samphat nai*), and rhyme between poetic units, or external rhyme (*samphat nok*), because rhyme appears in the text only at boundaries between hemistichs, lines, and stanzas. The very few possible counterexamples can convincingly be shown to appear in modern corruptions of the text. Also, many of the rhymes that appear in the text are used more than once, and some pairs or groups of rhyming syllables appear repeatedly. The words *chai* (heart), *dai* (any), and *nai* (in), for example, appear twelve times as the required three-element rhyme pattern of *khlong si*.[32] Such repetition would probably have been avoided by poets working in a written tradition, but it would have been a valuable tool for poets in an oral one.

Parry also endeavors to demonstrate that there was no single author of the *Iliad*, which implies that any member of the speech community could have told the story, shaping it as individual preference and the local situation required, in a process that could have endured over long periods with an indeterminate number of storytellers. We can draw the same conclusions for the Phra Lo text. The Phra Lo story would have evolved, conceivably from a time well before the rise of Ayutthaya, passed on from generation to generation, until some external factor intervened and interrupted that process of oral transmission. Perhaps it was spontaneous language change that rendered the forms unsuitable for continued use, or perhaps the appearance of some form of writing technology gave rise to new techniques of storytelling, or possibly both, at which point the essential components of the story would have been recorded. What had been a living and evolving text, always told with individual variations, became fixed, at least in part, and variation would come to be seen as an unwelcome departure.

Lilit Phra Lo as a Story

In terms of structure, the plot of the tale develops in linear fashion and thus feels familiar to readers. Transitions, on the other hand, are seldom indicated, so it is often difficult to know when a time or a location has changed, and gaps in the plot are opened but then left unresolved—both aspects that are quite unlike a modern text. In terms of presentation, there is no definitive way to distinguish between the voice of the narrator and that of a character in the story, and there are no textual or orthographic devices with which to indicate speaker or addressee, or to distinguish between thought and speech. To account for such differences, let us first think of how texts are created now.

Modern texts are usually the work of a single author, or as with some poetic texts of the early Bangkok era, the work of a group of collaborators. Modern authors can assume that individual reading will be the primary method of encountering the text, and that the reader will rely on the author's presentation for every detail of the story, such as the time and setting, the identity of a speaker, the significance of events and objects in the text, and the resolution of all conflicts. The modern author will generally focus on a central theme or plot and will be sure that everything is related in some way to it. There is no extraneous detail. Once a character, plot development, or other detail appears, the reader can safely assume that it is significant and that its implications will be explained or resolved. Given these expectations shared by modern authors and readers, it is understandable that some aspects of the Phra Lo story are seen as problematic.

In the oral tradition that gave rise to the tale of Phra Lo, both performer and audience were familiar with the story, and all would have known the main points. The text would have been recited or sung, most likely along with a visual enactment of some kind such as puppetry that would have made clear such details as transitions in time or location, and the identity of the speaker. Rather than knowing the text from individual reading, the audience would have encountered it in performance, seeing it recreated frequently and over time, expecting and accepting variation with each telling.

The introduction of writing to such a culture probably proceeded along predictable lines. The linguist A. L. (Pete) Becker considered this issue during his studies in Burma and Indonesia and noted that the most necessary components of a good performance—those without which the main purpose of telling the story would not have been met—are the parts that would have been preserved in writing, in what he referred to as "plot books."[33] This is very much what the extant manuscript volumes of the Phra Lo story seem to be.[34] The extemporaneous portions of a performance, what we would think of today as ephemera, would not have been preserved.[35]

Although the classical repertoire as it is presented today in the National Theater in Bangkok is primarily in the form of dance, it is likely that the Phra Lo text grew out of the old and widespread tradition of shadow puppet theater.[36] Depicting the grand scenes of the story—the great royal procession, the battle scenes with both human and spirit combatants, the many elephants and knights, the great festival scenes, the enchanted forests, and so on—would have required enormous resources for a dance presentation but could have easily been accomplished with puppets. While puppet theater is no longer as popular as it once was in Southeast Asia, it is still known throughout the region and has even been the object of preservation efforts in Thailand. In a performance, the power of the storyteller's words combines with the cooperative imagination of the audience to bring grand spectacles vividly to life.[37]

Even as technology is changing the way society pursues entertainment, living memory reminds us of the vibrant traditions of oral performance and of extemporaneous storytelling in Thailand.[38] Troupes of singers and dancers were often hired to entertain villagers who came together to share the labor at harvest time. Marriage celebrations might include performance as entertainment. Annual fundraising events for local temples, as well as secular provincial fairs, often running for several consecutive nights, included performances of folk theater, in both Thai and Chinese, complete with music, singing, and costumed performers on portable stages. Funeral observances often included entertainment for mourners who gathered for lengthy vigils. Merit-making activities that include performance, whether a human audience is present or not, can still be seen in the heart of Bangkok at the Erawan Shrine. New versions of these activities still take place, and although technological innovation may have changed the method of delivery, classic tales remain a part of much television programming. Episodes and characters from the Indic Ramayana are commonly presented in the National Theater in Bangkok.

Performances with strong regional appeal have attracted audiences well into the present day.[39] Not many decades ago, while the reach of television was still limited, advertising was joined with public performance in an effort to develop the Thai consumer economy by blending traditional storytelling with modern technology. Traveling vendors were dispatched into rural areas, where they presented popular Thai and foreign films to draw viewers, who were potential customers for products such as condensed milk, mosquito repellent, laundry soap, and shampoo, among others, which they sold between reels of the films. Foreign-language films were not subtitled but instead were dubbed by a voice-over specialist, known as *nak phak* (นักพากย์], who provided dialogue for all the characters, frequently tailoring the story for the local audience and adding sly and humorous references to local concerns and personalities.

Some of these performance styles have been codified, with spontaneity reduced or eliminated entirely. This is especially true in formal settings such as the National Theater and in prerecorded broadcasts, but others clearly display a mixture of the stereotypical and the novel in which the structure of the story, the array of essential components, is repeated but the embellishment is ephemeral, tailored to the specific audience.

If *Lilit Phra Lo* was likewise once a story told repeatedly, easily embellished and adapted for specific audiences, the published form today is certainly not the entire story as it would have been known in performance, but a single version of its stereotypical components— essential portions of the story phrased to the satisfaction of whoever was first motivated to write it down. That written form may then have been used by succeeding generations of performers as a reminder of those essential, stereotypical building blocks of the story, but there still would likely have been added embellishments for each telling, shaped by the skill of the storyteller and tailored to fit the context.

Modern views of the text seem to have been based on assumptions about text creation that would have been unknown in earlier times. Contrary to such assumptions, the story was not composed by a single author who expected that it would be read, and is instead the product of many storytellers, presenting the story aloud to various audiences that had heard it presented previously many times, and knew its basics very well. As in today's living performance traditions of Southeast Asia, it would have been the ability to embellish the story each time that marked the most favored storytellers, who would entertain audiences by interjecting local references. It is also inevitable that even the essential portions of the story changed somewhat from presentation to presentation, and that it evolved over time.

Viewed from this perspective, what may appear to be weaknesses become inconsequential. The frequently expressed concern, for example, over hemistichs that exceed the expected five syllables, turns out to be a problem only if one is focusing exclusively on the text in print. Those same hemistichs when recited aloud by a practiced storyteller, can nearly always be easily resolved into five stressed syllables.

Lilit Phra Lo and Its Cultural Context

The details about the characters and the plot also reflect the society and the culture from which the story arose. We know, for example, that the verse forms used to tell the story are indigenous because they also appear, in analogous patterns, in sister languages of Thai.[40] Similar character names appear in stories that are told in some of those languages, so it seems reasonable to assume that the story is also indigenous, rather than being based on Indic models.[41] The struggle for preeminence among the Thai-speaking peoples of the area appears only in the introductory stanzas, which celebrate the glories of a triumphant Ayutthaya, and is not mentioned elsewhere in the story; this makes it likely that the story predates such concerns and that those stanzas were prepended at a later date. The clear indications that the story is the product of an oral tradition and that it developed through repeated retellings raise the possibility that its origins may predate even the founding of that city.

Turning to the plot of the story, we learn of two estimable kingdoms, equally wealthy and powerful, and each ruled by a valorous king surrounded by a virtuous royal family. King Maensuang, who rules from his capital Suang, determines to attack and subdue King Phimphisakhonrat and his capital, known as Song. The attack is not successful, but King Phimphisakhonrat is killed in the conflict, creating lasting enmity between the two cities. In time, the royal Lo ascends the throne of Suang and rules as king. In Song, meanwhile, two royal daughters, princesses named Phuean and Phaeng, hear descriptions of Phra Lo and become enchanted. They turn for help to their two ladies-in-waiting, Ruen and Roy, who arrange for descriptions of the sisters to be carried to Suang, where Phra Lo hears them and in turn becomes enchanted. Eventually magic is employed to bring these three together, much of it controlled by a powerful, if enigmatic, adept named Samingphrai. Eventually the three are united, after a difficult and ill-omened journey undertaken by Phra Lo, who is accompanied by his two attendants, Kaew and Khwan. The four attendants become lovers, as do the three royals, and when they couple, which is presented in elaborate metaphorical passages, their passion has an enlivening impact on all the world. Finally, vengeful trickery brings about a covert attack in which all of them, first the four gallant attendants and then the three great royals, willingly embrace fate and so come to their final end. The three royal figures are bloodied and pierced by poisoned arrows, but their corpses fall against each other and remain in a standing position, still lifelike and regal. They are at first mourned but then for their valor and dignity are celebrated in both cities, which out of respect and admiration, embrace amity and peace.

The plot is not a complex one, but there are significant aspects to it and to the presentation of the story that are worth considering in detail for what they suggest about the ideas and concerns of those who created and developed the story. Power and the manipulation of power in a variety of ways are important throughout the story and are convenient points from which to view the story as a whole.

Military Power

The events of the story begin in stanza 7 of the modern published editions, with the King of Suang stating his intention to subjugate the King of Song. He gives no motivation for his decision to go to war; he does not suggest that he has been offended by his rival or that he fears his rival's ambitions. Nor is mention made of a conflict of the type that appears in the invocation, which was probably added at a later date and in which rivalries are expressed in real-world ethnic terms. Instead, the decision to seek domination is left unmotivated, suggesting that the expectation of the time was simply that this is what a powerful king does. Troops are then gathered and an attack is launched. It is ultimately unsuccessful, but both Suang and Song exercise military power through their armies, and while the description of the conflict is brief it evokes an image of fierce warfare. When, in due course, Phra Lo prepares for his own journey, a great entourage is assembled, the description of which leaves no doubt of the massive earthly power that awaits his bidding (stanza 228–30).

Magic Power

The sorcerer Samingphrai exercises power of a different sort. He demonstrates his control over nature by first conjuring a terrifying jungle with a threatening array of birds, mammals, reptiles, and spirits, all of ill omen, that serve to terrify the two palace ladies who are traveling to him to beg for his intercession on behalf of the royal princesses. His power is further shown when he replaces the threatening jungle with a benign forest, filled with beautiful flowering trees, and peaceful animals and birds, arrayed in scenes of idyllic beauty. He again demonstrates his power, beginning in stanza 144, by summoning all manner of demonic beings to assemble into an overwhelmingly powerful army, which he sends to attack the defending spirits of Suang. But perhaps the most striking marker of his power is his ability to alter both the forms and the cycle of life itself; first changing the tigers who stand guard over him into beautiful cats, he then performs a more amazing transformation of himself, appearing to the ladies at first as a wizened sage, then a comely youth, then a fully mature adult. In short, he has power over all of life, in every dimension and kind. The only limit to his power, we learn in stanza 83, is the inevitability of karma over which he has no control.

Interestingly, these exercises of magical power take place outside of the city environment, as though the outer world is a fertile place for such activities. We do learn of such power having an impact within the confines of the city when Lady Bunluea, the mother of Phra Lo, repeatedly gathers practitioners of all the magical arts to minister to her son, but the tale does not locate their activities inside the city itself.

Power as Display

More mundane power is also prominently displayed. Phra Lo begins his personal preparation for his journey (stanza 224–27) as he first bathes and then dons his royal regalia, the description of which shows him to be the epitome of regal splendor. The depictions of the magnificent entourage that accompanies him on his journey, as well as the descriptions of the great ceremonies arranged by both cities toward the end of the story, convey a sense of immense royal power and grandeur. The presentation brings to mind the concept of the theater state put forth by Clifford Geertz.[42] The nature of such a state is expressed through pageantry, he says, with its "expressive nature ... pointed ... toward spectacle, toward ceremony, toward the public dramatization of status pride." Geertz was, of course, studying an actual event in the recent history of Bali rather than a poetic text from centuries ago in Thailand, but his conclusion seems easily applicable to the Phra Lo story, reflecting something of the conceptual world of storytellers of long ago.

Language as Power

Another kind of power appears most obviously in the catalogs of trees, flowers, birds, and animals, in which the poet demonstrates a sort of power over the natural world by naming living beings within it. Beginning in stanza 71, for example, as the two ladies-in-waiting, Ruen and Roy, travel through the deep forest passes, the narrator's voice names what they see, beginning with the grasses and trees, grouping them by alliteration and by rhyme. In stanza 72, as they move deeper into the forest they see primates and predators, large mammals, snakes, and finally owls, with all the suggestion of the ill omen that they carry, again linked by alliteration and rhyme. Each listing becomes more elaborate than the last, until what had been simple phrases develops into complex catalogs of nature.

Subsequent catalogs become far more elaborate, going beyond simple lists of similar items by mixing types of living beings and linking them together with sound play. At one point in the text, for example, we see Phra Lo on his journey, passing through a forest, the description of which includes many of these more elaborate catalogs. In stanza 258, birds are associated with trees with homophonous names. In stanza 259 crows land in, pass above, or turn away from different trees that rhyme with *ka*, the Thai word for crow. Stanza 261 describes monkeys, *ling* in Thai, playing in the trees. Of the 32 syllables that make up the stanza, 31 of them begin with the *l* sound, in the most elaborate alliteration in the text. Stanza 262 consists of more than 40 tree and plant names linked together, as in other catalogs, by alliteration and rhyme. Some stanzas mix animals and plants with similar names, as in stanza 260, in which "the tiger crept past the 'tiger's eye' tree," and so on. In stanza 255, flowers begin to remind the king of what he has left behind, as "the 'lady's smile' flower is like my dear lady's smile of happiness."[43]

The catalogs employ masterful control of sound manipulation to demonstrate encyclopedic knowledge of nature. And while the catalogs may have been intended to demonstrate power expressed through language, language itself is presented as an instrument of power— most notably to enchant. In one such instance, the princesses Phuean and Phaeng are driven to distraction simply by hearing descriptions of Phra Lo. The measure of their discomfort is taken in stanza 30, in which the princesses rebuke their attendants, who, they seem to say, have been ignorant of a general infatuation with Phra Lo throughout the city of Song, brought on simply by the descriptions. In Suang, Phra Lo subsequently hears descriptions of the princesses and is similarly distressed because he can neither see them nor be with them. Descriptions then can have great power; more formidable still are the spells that the magician Samingphrai employs to bring Phra Lo to the princesses Phuean and Phaeng.

Sexuality as Power

Sexuality becomes the most important power in the story; it is expressed always in metaphorical terms but is unmistakable nonetheless, and although that sexuality has sometimes been decried, it is too significant to the text to be reduced to mere licentiousness. Sexual attraction, desire, and activity are presented in elaborate metaphors that include elements of the natural world: lotus blossoms of various colors, bees, beetles, birds, fish, bodies of water, rain, trees, and so on. All the major characters of the story engage in sexual play that is depicted in vivid if veiled terms. The couplings begin when the two sets of attendants, Kaew and Khwan, who serve Phra Lo, and Ruen and Roy, who serve the princesses Phuean and Phaeng, encounter each other for the first time in the princesses' pleasure garden, where they pair off and couple (stanza 398–422). The descriptions are filled with elaborate metaphors depicting the four of them as very young and very beautiful, embodying every refinement that palace life can impart upon one who is called upon to serve royals who are themselves the epitome of all that is good and admirable.

When Phra Lo and the two princesses finally meet in the same pleasure garden they also engage in rapturous coupling, during which they are even more vigorous than were their attendants (stanza 516–36). These descriptions, too, are couched in elaborate metaphor, but it is clear that the three of them are physically perfect, and endowed with all refinements, are very young and sexually very strong, and that it is Phra Lo, as the divine king, who is the most vigorous of all.[44] The attention to sexual prowess is suggestive of concepts of Hinduism in which the lingam and yoni represent the generative power of nature expressed and experienced in sexual union.

Much of the story has been setting the scene for this meeting. The plot events and the depictions of the characters have created a vividly imagined world, a world of two kingdoms that are peopled with individuals of such perfection that they blend the mundane and the divine. The king and the princesses are often likened to the sun and the moon and are repeatedly described as gods incarnate. With all the divine attributes ascribed to them throughout the story, when they finally meet we cannot escape the implication that they are, in fact, divinities meeting in human form. Their first encounter is so powerful (stanza 493–94) that the princesses momentarily set aside the norms of customary formality as the three of them stare unblinkingly at one another. The princesses "forgot themselves, and met the king's gaze," and in the following stanza we learn that Phra Lo, in turn, gazes at them in a rapture of his own. The four attendants then are transfixed by the scene before them, as they gaze on these apparent divinities, a reaction that they must struggle to overcome in order to preserve propriety. All become enraptured in gazing, as though sharing of themselves through the act of seeing.

Thus, the subsequent passages depicting the sexual coupling of the king and the two princesses are not expressions of romantic sentiment or of simple physical gratification but are an expression of a shared human and divine potency, a fructifying power experienced in a generative act of procreation that enlivens the world around them. Nature responds to their powerful joining (stanza 537–40) as thunder sounds through the heavens, the seas are stirred to foam, forests are shaken, and animals engage their partners in lovemaking. In these passages the poem becomes an expression of fertility, a pure generative power, and a life force of a merged human and divine perfection that passes to all the world.

Heroic Power

Much of the story of Phra Lo is reminiscent of mythological motifs in the foundation stories of many cultures around the world. The journey that Phra Lo undertakes, for example, fits easily into the concept of the "hero's journey" as described by Joseph Campbell in his comparative studies of mythology.[45] When Phra Lo reaches the Kalong River he faces the decision of whether to press on or to abandon the journey and return to his own city, there to rule in safety and comfort. He is clearly suffering, torn between his love for those he has left behind and the attraction of those who await his arrival (stanza 286–302). As part of his deliberation he seeks an omen in the waters, which swirl threateningly and turn deep red, showing him that his journey will end in tragedy. He is deeply burdened by this knowledge, so burdened that he sheds tears of blood. He steels himself, though, and continues on, lest he be ridiculed for cowardice. But soon he again hesitates, at which point a beautiful forest cock, possessed by a spirit sent by the powerful Samingphrai, comes to lure him ever deeper into the hostile kingdom—thus performing the role of what Campbell identifies as a guide to the venturing hero.

The hoped-for return from the hero's journey is not part of Phra Lo's fate, however; like the towering heroes we see in the mythologies that lie at the base of the world's great belief systems, a figure intervenes, and in this case with treachery. However the intervention might be described, a seemingly inevitable worldly victory is at first thwarted, but the hero then demonstrates a capacity for greatness far beyond mortals. In the Phra Lo story the intervention comes from the princesses' grandmother who, in her unending rage over the military attack on the city of Song that begins the tale, tricks her troops into an assault. The seven royals and attendants face death without fear preferring instead to die with dignity, certain of a future rebirth to rule in a heavenly kingdom. (stanza 602) In so doing they show that all truly possessed the virtues of a great king and his retinue. All accept their sacrificial role willingly as they choose to accord themselves perfectly with their station and duties in life. The resulting grief experienced in the two rival cities, moreover, and the great respect generated by the display of royal character, reconcile the leaders of the two cities, who forswear violence and embrace peace.

Campbell points out that the hero's journey often involves a great boon derived by a successful struggle. In this tale the benefit is restoration of peace between the two kingdoms, earned at the great cost of the deaths of the royal children and their attendants. The depiction of the three royals standing together in death, leaning into each other in a lifelike tableau makes it clear that they have transcended human limitations. In their dignified death they make themselves complete; by choosing neither to fear nor to flee, they embrace the most royal of virtues. And in death they correct an imbalance created by unbridled ambition and resulting in such enmity that resolving it demanded the highest possible sacrifice.

It is significant that the characters' acceptance of death takes place shortly after their sexual couplings. Campbell's analysis of world mythology shows that often a sacrifice of the foremost youth of a community either at or soon following a sexual coupling is seen as bringing fertility to the world.[46] In the tale of Phra Lo the couplings have quickened and enlivened nature, and the sacrifice returns peace and stability to a world thrown out of balance by the unmotivated war that set all in motion.

In the invocation of the poem, the four stanzas that form a paean to Ayutthaya evoke a real-world struggle for dominance in a specific region that is out of keeping with the world conjured up by the tale. This world of Phra Lo lies beyond the mundane considerations of normal life and exists instead in a mythological realm that represents all of the cosmos. The stanzas that have been added to the tale, the first four and the last two of the story as we know it today, fit the needs of the rising capital city of Ayutthaya, but before they were added to it the story served a far more expansive purpose. Had circumstances been different the tale of Phra Lo might have developed into the foundation story of an empire even greater than Ayutthaya, with Phra Lo taking a place like that of the hero figures of the great myths of India. This is not to claim a special position for the tale but to attempt to locate it in a larger world of storytelling, with its earliest roots extending deeply into the past—perhaps even to a time before the world religions spread throughout the globe, when cultures established from within themselves those beliefs on which they would develop. It is possible to speculate that, had Hinduism and subsequently Buddhism not reached Southeast Asia, the story of a hero named Lo might have spread throughout all the Thai-speaking domain and been recognized as a foundation myth for all of them. It is, at the very least, an intriguing possibility.

Campbell's work also suggests an explanation for one puzzling detail of the Phra Lo story that is unexplained within the text, and that is the presence of two princesses in the story. Phra Phuean and Phra Phaeng are not differentiated in any significant way and nothing explains why there should be two of them. Although there is no explanation, the presence of the two characters requires an elaboration of the scene in which the royal coupling is presented, as Phra Lo is said to have been equally vigorous with both—a detail that suggests there was an important reason why each woman must participate in the generative act. Campbell points out that some mythologies include two women, sometimes twins, as main characters representing two cultural patterns, one based on hunting and the other based on planting.[47] It is tempting to think that such a blending of ancient patterns was intended by those who first told the tale as they faced the challenges of developing cultural patterns that were suitable for city life. Such a blending would suggest that the roots of the story extend back very far indeed in the development of what would become the dominant cultural pattern that would eventually give rise to the Kingdom of Ayutthaya. Perhaps study of the mythologies of other members of the Thai family may one day help determine if such associations are implicit in the Phra Lo story.

Social Context

The story of Phra Lo is sometimes included among texts said to be Buddhist in nature, suggesting that identifiably Buddhist customs, themes, values, or the like are to be found within it. A close examination of the text, however, suggests a clearer affinity with Hinduism, which preceded Buddhism in Southeast Asia and which dominated those areas ruled by the Kingdom of Angkor, including large areas of modern Thailand prior to the rise of Ayutthaya.

Throughout the text the main royal characters are frequently identified with Hindu deities. Stanza 11, for example, tells that "[Phra Lo] was as Indra, descending like a shower of raindrops from the heavens, God incarnate for people to admire." In the Vedic texts Indra has mastery over the heavens, and rain is a gentle and beneficial aspect of that mastery. In the following stanzas, Phra Lo is compared with the moon and associated with the "God of love," or Vishnu. The two princesses, for their part, are also associated with the Hindu pantheon. In stanza 37, "The two are as heavenly raindrops descending to the earth, beautiful as nymphs of Indra, come to the world." When these characters finally meet in stanza 493, their mutual admiring gaze, which both they and their attendants are hard pressed to break, calls to mind the concept of Hinduism known as *darsan*, the encountering of divinity through sight. In this, "a prolonged look is a means of expressing . . . and of participating in the essence and nature" of the object of the gaze. Having shared their essence and nature in this way, the three then unite physically in the so-called "miracle passages" beginning with stanza 537. These passages, and those that describe the coupling of the pairs of attendants, are evocative of a fertility mythology that is in keeping with Hinduism, and may well have had even older local roots.

There are also many smaller details that seem in keeping with Hinduism. For example, in her frantic efforts to help Phra Lo resist the magic that has been used against him, Lady Bunluea turns to Sitthichai, a skilled magician and master of spells and potions who undertakes a fire ceremony and offers sacrifices (stanza 139). When all her efforts prove futile, Phra Lo takes leave of his mother and sets out on his journey. Her deep fears unassuaged, she seeks divine intervention to ensure his safety:

I entrust my child to all the divinities, guardians of the earth,
of the air, of the trees, of the waters and of the vast jungles.
Shiva, Vishnu, Indra, and Brahma,
help to protect the Elephant Lord. Keep him from danger. (201)

In artistic expression both Buddhism and monarchy in Thailand have retained much of Hindu cosmology and mythology, albeit in a position subservient to the triumph of the Buddha himself. Nonetheless, these passages seem more in keeping with a worldview grounded in Hinduism.

Similarly, it is interesting to note that Phra Lo is a great king because he is born that way. He is compared frequently to Vishnu, the sun, and the moon, and his physical beauty is described in elaborate detail. His greatness is not due to great deeds or significant accomplishments, but to his very nature. Throughout the text there is a blending of aspects of divinity and kingship that would seem to have more in common with the Khmer concept of the *devaraja*, or god-king, than with the later Kingdom of Ayutthaya and the concept of the *dharmaraja*, or meritorious king.

Regarding the language, some of the vocabulary that is not Thai in origin is Indic, as might be expected of a classical text, in line with the conventions of the more familiar *Ramakian*, the Thai retelling of the Ramayana epic. There is also a significant component of vocabulary that is easily identified as Khmer in origin. The great magician who appears in the tale, for example, is known as "Samingphrai," a name that is composed of two elements, the first of which, *saming* (lord, king; tiger), is from Mon, a language related to Khmer. And much of the everyday vocabulary is also derived from Khmer. The story and the verse forms are completely Thai and owe nothing to borrowing, but the Khmer element is large enough to call for further consideration.

While each of these points is relatively small, they take on a greater importance when considered together. The text is certainly Thai in origin, but these details suggest the possibility that the intellectual environment at some point in the development of the tale was heavily influenced by Khmer language and thought, which would not have been surprising to find prior to or in the early years of Ayutthaya.

On Translating *Lilit Phra Lo*

In this translation I follow the page format and the sequential numbering used in the Ministry of Education edition.[48] A few stanzas that appear in the manuscript volumes have been omitted without comment from the ministry text; these I have inserted into the translation along with explanatory endnotes, without changing the numbering of subsequent stanzas. I have followed the line and spacing conventions of printed editions to facilitate comparison between the translation and the Thai wording.

It did not seem either possible or wise to attempt to replicate rhyme patterns found in the Thai verse, or to have presented the story in English poetic forms, both of which approaches have been advocated by some Thai writers. Previous attempts along these lines have not seemed promising,[49] and I beg the indulgence of those who have argued to the contrary.[50]

While I could not see a way to replicate in translation the poetic features of the original, it did seem appropriate to reflect, as much as was possible, the content of each five-syllable hemistich. Nearly always throughout the text, each one is syntactically separate from and independent of other such units, as is particularly striking in the stanzas of *khlong si*. For these stanzas I have regarded the shorter two- and four-syllable hemistichs, which are not syntactically separate or independent, as *kham soi*, or "decorative passages," and included them within the larger unit. Phrasing the translation in this way seems to me to preserve an important part of the verse forms used to tell the story; the dominance of the hemistich is, I believe, an important echo of the oral tradition that first gave life to the story.[51] One result of preserving the hemistich in this way is the need to deal with a significant degree of repetition, especially of the titles and epithets that are used so frequently in oral epic poetry, which is not to favored in English verse. On the other hand, eliminating the hemistich structure and thereby avoiding the undesirable repetition results, in my hands at least, in very spare English prose that has the feel of a précis more than of a translation.

While I have thus followed much of the format found in the Ministry of Education edition, I have attempted to follow the content of the manuscript volumes of the text that are now housed in the National Library of Thailand. In the early 1980s I requested and received microfilm copies of all fifty-four extant manuscript volumes of the story, which I subsequently collated, with the enthusiastic assistance of the Thai-language majors of Chiang Mai University. They painstakingly cut apart photocopies of each passage from each of the manuscript volumes and then pasted these onto a single sheet, numbering each version appropriately to show the source. The result is a full copy of the text, each hemistich on its own sheet topped by the wording of the Ministry of Education edition, with every version of that hemistich displayed underneath.[52] I have followed this compilation for all my subsequent study of the text and have included in this translation explanatory endnotes for passages in which the manuscript wording differs significantly from the printed wording.

Finally, where the text does not clearly indicate the identity of a speaker or addressee, I have inserted this information in brackets as an aid to the reader.

Lilit Phra Lo

INVOCATION

Glorious! Triumphant! Supreme! Oh mighty city, towering on high, reaching the lofty firmaments! All the earth, awed by your grandeur, trembles in fear of your power, conquering all in every direction. Attacking, laying waste to royal capitals, you put to the sword the Lao Kao,[53] severing their heads, scattering their corpses. You crush the Yuan, and the Lao you destroy, sending all fleeing[54] before you. Victorious, the Thai return in glory to their vast territory, the populace exulting in the triumph and the great royal treasury growing in glory. Throughout the far-flung frontiers the subjects rejoice, and happiness fills the earth. Oh great royal city, Ayutthaya, ornament of all the world, nine-jeweled[55] capital, city of splendor, standing above all, your merit overflows the sky! (1)

> Your meritorious king enlivens all the world,
> Multiplying exhilaration and bliss.
> Oh joyous Ayutthaya, incomparable and beyond description,
> All nations admire you, singing your praises. (2)

> Fully versed, oh men and women,
> I will regale you with the poem of Phra Lo, surpassing man,
> A euphonious narration of the utmost beauty,

fit for the lilting pipe and beguiling to the heart. (3)

Felicitous recitation, what could be its equal?
Feel its rhythm—what could compare?
A polished poem, told with artistry, soothes the heart.
Oh royal meritorious one, to you I present my tale. (4)[56]

THE STORY OF KING LO

I tell of a glorious leader, bold and daring as a god. Maensuang[57] was his name, a great noble of towering stature, lord of the magnificent city of Suang. His royal queen, a great lady of exceeding virtue, bore the name Bunluea. Beautiful courtesans served him in every position, and able ministers crowded about him. Elephants and horses he possessed in great abundance, and the troops at his command swarmed over the earth. Great companies of bold warriors teemed about him, and many vassal cities magnified his renown. He had a regal son, by name Phra Lo, one descended from the skies. It was in the west[58] that his territory lay. (5)[59]

And there was a great lord, king of the city of Song, who bore the name Phimphisakhonrat.[60] The treasures of the two kings were equally vast. This noble king to the east, replete with honor and dignity, had a royal son of illustrious power, by name Lord Phichaiphitsanukon.[61] When this son came of age, the king sent emissaries to seek the hand of Princess Darawadi, a beautiful lady of royal lineage, that she might become queen for his son. And so the son obtained a loving wife, charming and pleasing to the eye. After a time children were born to them, Phuean and Phaeng,[62] regal and beloved, in form and figure beautiful as the moon. Wherever one's gaze fell, there was beauty to arrest the heart, beauty beyond description. (6)

And then the great Lord Maensuang summoned his vassals to come and lay out plans, saying, "The city of Song has a bold monarch. Do not hesitate, for we shall make war and seize his territory and make him our vassal. Make haste and order my forces prepared!" The ministers convened and, when all was as he had ordered, the king joined the formations proceeding forth from the royal city. The companies of troops spread out, moving without hesitation onto the field of battle. The crush of soldiers, and elephants, and horses weighed heavily on the face of the earth. (7)

The great King Phimphisakhonrat, hearing that King Maensuang had brought a great army, sent his own troops out to meet them, arrayed in abundant ranks. And he himself went out without hesitation. The forward troops clashed together, brandishing swords, slashing, clanging; brandishing sabers, striking, hacking. Javelins flew in profusion, hurled in each direction. On the left, they fought without retreating; on the right, they fought without withdrawing. The bold against the bold, they reached out to slay. The daring against the daring, they grasped to conquer. They mixed together, thrusting and stabbing. Pressing together, they struggled in making war, calling out loudly for victory. Explosions echoed, shaking the field of battle. Crossbows fired in great numbers. Powerful longbows spewed forth arrows. The strong against the strong, they raised their arms to strike. Elephants met elephants, crashing together. Horses reared up amid the melee, joining the fray, their riders thrusting lances at the enemy. Pressing powerfully into the thick of the battle they reached Phimphisakhonrat, who perished astride his elephant. His officers interposed themselves and continued the fight, protecting their monarch's remains. They fled back to the city, and when the royal corpse was safely inside, they threw home the bolt, locking the gates. (8)

Lord Phichaiphitsanukon took up the rule of the royal capital. Lord Maensuang returned to rule his own city, and Lord Phichai stood in control of his territory. When he had performed the rites for his royal father, he bade the two young princesses go reside with their grandmother in her palace, together with two bright and clever ladies-in-waiting on whom he bestowed the pleasing names Ruen and Roy.[63] And so, the princesses betook themselves to their abode. (9)

At that time, Lord Maensuang, great and distinguished noble, sent to request the hand of the beautiful Lady Laksanawadi,[64] to be installed as principal queen for Phra Lo, along with a retinue of royal concubines in each office and every position. And it came to pass that this royal king and father took up residence in the heavenly realm, and Phra Lo assumed the sovereignty of the kingdom. The earth and skies paid unceasing praise to him, more beautiful than any earthly lord. (10)

> He was as Indra, descending like a shower of raindrops from the
>   heavens,
> god incarnate for people to admire. (11)

> He was trim and slender,
> elegant of waist, and graceful. In every feature a beautiful lord. (12)

> In shape, he surpassed all throughout the three realms:[65]

surpassing beauty; thoroughgoing beauty, beauty to entrance the
   heart. (13)

And his fame spread throughout the earth.
Every wandering trader spoke in praise of his comeliness. (14)

A lustrous moon enlightens a cloudless sky.
If one has not seen his face, look instead upon that moon, for they
   are as one! (15)

His eyes were those of the golden deer.
To look upon his eyebrow was to see a precious bow, flexed into a
   graceful arc. (16)

To gaze upon his radiant ear
was to gaze upon the petal of a precious lotus, and his cheek was like
   the golden plum.[66] (17)

The curve of his nose
was as if formed by the gods, like the hook of the god of love.[67] (18)

His royal lips, lovelier than any carving,
Were fresh and pretty, ready to smile. Oh, lovely and beautiful were
   his lips. (19)

Gaze upon his beautiful chin. Gaze upon his rounded neck, as
though fashioned on a lathe.[68] His shoulders evoked desire. His
breast beautiful as that of the god of love. His royal arms graceful
as the trunk of a pachyderm, his fingers lovely, the nails unequaled.
Excellence in every feature of his body, from royal feet to the tip of

the topknot, from the hair of the royal head, all the way to the feet—
all was beauty. The lordly king was beautiful[69] in every way. (20)

In every city, they sang the praises of the king
and told of illustrious Phra Lo throughout the land.
The appearance of this excellent youth overwhelmed the hearts of
the world.
Young men and women, upon hearing of him, were crazed and
reduced to lamentation. (21)

Praise of the lord's form was repeated throughout the city of Song,
carrying the news to the ears of the two sisters,
who languished there like a golden vine,[70] sighing in desire to look
upon him,
moaning mournfully in their chambers, longing for further word of
him.[71] (22)

Phra Phaeng and Phra Phuean were overwhelmed.
In their hearts, they dwelt only upon the lord.
They even imagined that they could see him and so were
bewildered.
Their breasts were inflamed and their faces downcast. (23)

Ruen and Roy went up to attend them
and saw the princesses immersed in gloom, as though stricken by
fever.
"You are always fresh and lovely as the moon.
Whence this despair? We beseech you, please, tell us. We wish to
know." (24)

[Phuean and Phaeng replied,] "If fever stems from illness, treatment
easily cures it.

With a bodily fever, anyone could help us.

Afflicted, though, with a fever of the heart, it is better that we die.

Consider this and make ready for our cremation." (25)

What the ladies-in-waiting heard left them speechless.

"Oh princesses, what can you mean by this?" (26)

"Why are you so vexed, revered ones?

Please, entrust it to us." (27)

[Phuean and Phaeng replied] "Our pain overflows the kingdom,
stranger than anything throughout the earth. If we told you, where
should we hide our faces, and who could help us in our mortification?
We fear we would be ridiculed, and we would more gladly die. Oh,
don't question us so. Our pain surpasses speech. Have pity on us and
add not to our affliction, lest we perish." (28)

The ladies-in-waiting[72] raised their hands in salutation, rededicating
their lives to the princesses. "We are your intimate and trusted
servants. Why do you have no faith in us, even so much as the weight
of a strand of hair? Oh princesses, have you no pity on us?" (29)

[Phuean and Phaeng:] "What are all these tales and rumors about?

Who is everyone praising throughout the earth?

Have you two slept so deeply that you've forgotten to awake?

Determine for yourselves what is wrong—don't ask us." (30)[73]

[Ruen and Roy replied,] "Oh, Dear Princesses, be not aggrieved.

We will take this task upon ourselves.

Somehow the king will come to unite[74] with you.

We'll find a way to send a message to him." (31)

[Phuean and Phaeng replied,] "It would be a shameful breach of
  custom

for a female to entice a male into her home.

Oh, with such pain, surely, we would be better off dead.

We love the king, but he does not even know of us." (32)

[Ruen and Roy replied,] "You are mistaken! This can be done.

We will devise a pleasing plan.

We will seek out powerful sorcerers

to entice the lord here in secret. How could he resist?" (33)

Inwardly the two ladies were thankful but outwardly feigned
disapproval and forbade the plan as a grievous wrong. "Your idea
is not a good one. We fear that people will learn of it and we will
be sullied. Our error would be known throughout the earth. Where
could we hide our faces?" But the ladies-in-waiting read their hearts
correctly and saw the ruse. [Ruen and Roy to each other said,] "These
royal hearts have not gone astray. We will do what must be done to
arrange what they pine for. Let the consequences fall upon us." To
the princesses they said, "You need know nothing of this. Leave it all
to us, for now we understand. If we are not to follow our ideas, why
would you keep us as your ladies-in-waiting?" (34)

"We will rely only on our intimates, upon whom we can depend.
We'll have them go trading along the waterways and travel about
on foot, proclaiming your beauty all through the city of Phra Lo.

They will praise you in song and story, telling of the royal princesses,
incomparable in their glory." (35)

"Every city has royal children, [they'll say,] and in great numbers,
but none compare with these two princesses:
Phra Phaeng, with majesty and beauty beyond all reckoning,
and Phra Phuean, in bearing and beauty as the orb of the moon. (36)

"The two are as heavenly raindrops descending to the earth,[75]
beautiful as nymphs of Indra, come to the world.
Don't long for, don't yearn for such beauties; they are beyond reach.
Just admire, with beatific smile, these meritorious royal offspring. (37)

"All you nobles and lords, and rulers of great cities,
Do not allow desire to beset you, for your love will consume you.
Stores of merit have sent these two radiant ones,
These two princesses, worthy of a king of supreme merit." (38)

Praise of the princesses
Was spoken throughout every dominion and domain, and King Lo
    heard the news. (39)

Hearing the songs, the exalted one
bade the singers brought to his audience hall. (40)

Hearing word of the young ones,
the great king lamented, overwhelmed. (41)

He thought secretly to himself,

"If I have truly have attained great merit, I will go to unite with you
  princesses." (42)

The great king was moved and praised the news of the sisters. He
bestowed rewards of clothing and garments. "Thank you for bringing
this news to me; it touches my heart." (43)

[He wondered,] "However am I going
to unite with these beautiful young women?" (44)

The lord then plaited verses about them,
poetry that was pleasing beyond compare. (45)

"Hearing the descriptions of you, told with such care,
I seem to see your beauty with my very eyes.
Oh, my glorious, perfect ones, golden lotuses,
lay on each side of me, your flesh pressed close to mine."[76] (46)

He placed one hand against his forehead,[77]
and with the other he stroked his breast, purposely allowing them to
  see. (47)

Following this pretense, he provided for them in proper measure.
Refreshed, they then took leave of him to return to their city. There
they went to inform Ruen and Roy of every detail. And the ladies-
in-waiting then told the princesses every detail of what had come
about. (48)

They then sought out a sorceress and came upon a maker of potions,
one of great power, and highly skilled. They told her all in detail

and said, "If you help us accomplish our goal we will repay you handsomely and give you ample rewards. And when Phra Lo unites with the princesses, you will have bounty beyond compare." (49)

> She heard them out but shook her head.
> "I can entice only low-born men.
> For me to tempt a celestial lord would be to no avail, my dear
> > ones." (50)

> [Ruen and Roy replied,] "Then who do you know whose skills you
> > respect?
> Please tell us clearly, and we will go ourselves." (51)

She said, "I know all of the other practitioners. They are inept, hapless. There are only three of us who are seasoned, powerful masters of spirits. Whomever we beckon will come. Whomever we seek will come, save only for a celestial lord, ruler of the earth. Such a one is knowledgeable and is well versed,[78] possessing power and merit and qualities far beyond ours. We cannot charm such a king. It is completely beyond us." (52)

"And so, of those I know, there are three with undoubted power. All have mastered the arts of magic, and all are pupils of the revered Samingphrai. But when they reached the pathway, she left them. The two of them then went in to the venerable and powerful adept.[79] Making offerings, they related all the details to him, begging for help in their difficulty. But the practitioner responded as the sorceress had, saying, "Our rank is too low, and we can entice only those of our own kind, who are subject to the power of spirits and of magic spells. But a universal lord, who could hope to overcome such a figure?" The two ladies were aggrieved by what they heard, saying, "Compassionate sir, you know those with rank and standing, with magical power and authority. To whoever succeeds in drawing him here we will assure massive gain, a fortune in gold. So also will we reward whoever merely points us to that exalted master. So please tell us quickly, that we may be able to recognize him." (53)

The practitioner said, "Beneath the heavens and in all the earth, who could hope to compare with, who could be the equal of, the venerable lord Samingphrai? He says, 'Die!' and death comes before one's eyes. He says, 'Live!' and life comes, in that instant. Whomever he beckons comes. Whomever he seeks cannot stay away. If you wish to see him, I will take you there. But the way is very far. At evening you ladies return home, and hurry back with tomorrow's dawn." The two ladies took leave of the practitioner to go inform the princesses, who were well pleased. (54)

> The two princesses, lovely ones, received this news
> as though hearing that the king was about to set out.
> And, as when the shining sun brings the lotus into bloom, they were
>   filled with freshness
> but still were fearful lest the matter spread and become known to
>   others. (55)

> The two of them resorted to clever evasion,
> hiding all with pretense and deception.
> They concealed their excitement with artful ruse,
> disguising their delight, making the strange and improper seem
>   good. (56)[80]

The ladies-in-waiting saw the artifice and they were pleased,
and they then placed deceit upon deception.
Going to attend the noble grandmother they asked, "Have you seen
your royal granddaughters?
The two are in great distress, pale of face and sorrowful of eye. (57)

"A seer has told us to call their souls, [81]
which have dispersed to the far reaches of the sky,
ventured throughout the land to the mountains and the forests and
the fields.
He said, 'Call their souls back without delay; the morning of
tomorrow is an auspicious time.'" (58)

The grandmother heard this news with great distress.
"Hurry to inform the king,
their gallant, royal sire."
And so, the ladies-in-waiting went to attend their king and told him
all. (59)

Upon hearing them the king was sorely distressed.
"Whatever the practitioner wants, bring it quickly."
[Ruen and Roy reply] "Lord, we are to call their souls at the
mountain of the venerable one.
The practitioner told us to arrange for fast elephants." (60)

[The king replied,] "Go—make arrangements and then return
and inform my daughters."
Phuean and Phaeng listened happily to this news.
"Leave at dawn, dear ones, and be swift in aiding us." (61)

"Take the sleek elephant that we know as 'Like the Breeze,'
and the swift 'Lord of the Winds,' so aptly named.
Observe the admirable speed of their strides.
They are fast, and urged on are faster still, superbly swift." (62)

At cock's first crow the elephants were prepared
and brought forth, one to each side of the ladies' mounting
  platform(63)

And before dawn's first light Ruen and Roy instructed the
  princesses,
"Dress and prepare all in readiness in case our venerable lord should
  come." (64)

"We shall take our leave of you now, exalted ones.
Waiting here until the break of day would only delay us, and the way
  is long." (65)

They mounted the elephants and quickly set out, passing swiftly along
the pathways. When they had reached halfway, the venerable one saw
them coming and transformed himself into a wondrously comely
and beautiful youth.[82] And so they inquired after the venerable one,
who broke into a smile and laughed, replying, "From what domain
do you two come?" (66)

The two thought to themselves,
"Is this youth kin of the venerable one? Could any other be so
  comely? (67)

"But this is just a distraction of the God of Love.[83]

It would only delay us, and the princesses will be in distress." (68)

Soon, they saw it was the venerable one, his aged form appearing wondrous, and they were amazed by this realization. "Who could be your equal, venerable one? Please help the princesses. We need seek no further than here!" (69)

[The practitioner replied,] "Would you abandon a fire to blow on a glow worm?
 The power of my knowledge is limited." [Ruen and Roy answered,] "We just can't tell, can we?" (70)

Inviting the venerable practitioner to mount and ride with them, they drove the elephants to their limits, the three following one another along. Turning their faces to the green mountains, they gazed about them at the plains as they swiftly moved along. They gazed upon the ranges of the forested mountains, pushing through stands of tall grasses, *faek*, *khaem*, and *lao*. They went through thick forests of soaring *pradao* and *pradu* trees, through *yang* and *yung* trees, and *takhian*, tall as the floating mists, and *phayom*, with its flowers reaching to the clouds. There was a multitude of trees of many kinds, with branches encircled by embracing vines all setting new leaves as the breeze caressed their buds. Flowers sprouted forth in clusters like upraised hands offering nectar. Everywhere there were bountiful spreading blossoms and refreshing scents and ripening fruit. Young leaves and large full trunks, branches, and twigs all were beautiful. (71)[84]

And before long they reached the foothills of the mountains. There they saw monkeys, languor, lemurs, and gibbons calling out with dreadful ghostly sounds, and their hair stood on end in terror. Panthers crept up toward the pathway. Rhino and water buffalo lay blocking their path. Herds of gaur wandered the jungle. Wild bulls grazed the forest. Boars and bears[85] roamed about.

Countless herds of female elephants grouped together following the bulls. Hooded snakes sprayed deadly poisons, and pythons wrapped themselves tightly about buffalos. Antelope scaled the peaks and all manner of strange and dreadful creatures filled the high mountain recesses. But the practitioner was not troubled and pressed on, readily entering the jungle, and pushing rapidly along the way. (72)

Pity the two women, struck with fear. Their breasts trembled and shook, hearts pounding and trembling as though to burst. Hastily threading their way along, following the practitioner, they saw watercourses, swamps, and marshes, brooks and rivers and streams. Alligators in great numbers lay in wait, watching, their heads upraised, snatching at prey. Hippopotamus attacked, lunging at reflections. Mermaids dragged people beneath the waters, tumbling and grimacing, eyes wide in horror, dying, entangled in their own hair. Above them in the high treetops they heard the cries of *saek* and *ngao* and *ngut*, the soft complaint of the *thing thut*, and the cry of the nestling *khaoku*, their scolding echoing through the forest. Hearing this, too, they were struck with fear. The aged practitioner laughed as they went along, comforting them: "Do not be afraid. It really is nothing. All these things are merely the conjuring of the venerable one." The practitioner was in awe of nothing. Driving the elephants in haste toward the mountains, they went together without delay. As soon as they reached the foot of the mountains, the aged practitioner dismounted from the elephant. Leaving the two women at a distance he went on toward the venerable lord, Samingphrai. Reaching him, he made a deep obeisance and spoke of the royal princesses, the regal Phuean and golden Phaeng. (73)

"They are in difficulty equaling the sky,
and they sent offerings to me that I should bring their ladies-in-
waiting here." (74)

The venerable lord said, "Practitioner,
go and tell them not to fear but to draw close to me." (75)

The practitioner then came to tell the women,
"The venerable one bids you two enter. Please, go in." (76)

They saw tigers attending him on either side.[86]
And so, in fear and terror they prostrated, and entered. Bowing low,
they saluted him. (77)

They watched the unblinking tigers and saw them become cats with the most beautiful of markings. They stole glances at the venerable lord, who transformed his aged form, with its hair of pure white, eyebrows of white, and eye lashes without pigmentation. Before them he became a youth of exceedingly beautiful and fine proportions, attractively slender and tall, virile in bearing, and laughing with satisfaction. Then suddenly, and by his own power, he matured, taking on a pleasing appearance and tranquil bearing. The two gave him offerings of respect, which they had prepared in anticipation of this meeting. They then presented their message: "The princesses bow in salutation at the feet of our lord, who dwells among us." (78)

"Their suffering is as great as all the heavens.

They look to you and to you alone, our royal lord." (79)

"We have hastened here, traveling since first light.
and they bid us invite[87] you to release them from their suffering." (80)

"We invite your intercession, and when all is accomplished
we beg to present you great mounds of silver and of gold and
    countless precious stones." (81)

"They burn with intense desire.
Please, lord, help the princesses to escape death." (82)

The venerable one uttered not a word in response but remained
still for a time. He went into a trance, questioning, "Should I assist
them, or should I not?" And he saw all, every detail. Due to their old
karma, they had been at times attentive, at times lax. And so, that
which was to come about could not be averted. In keeping with their
karma, in the end, they would perish. But he also saw that they had
long striven to be constant in their merit making, always seeking his
protection. He then emerged from his trance and said, "Speak not to
me of payments or of bribes! I will go to the dwelling place of the
two princesses. You two go before me and relate this news for them
to hear. I will follow without delay. If not today, then tomorrow will
I arrive." (83)

Greatly pleased, they received his words with salutations, saying in
reply, "Your words are as a hundred vessels of celestial water poured
down in a soothing bath of comfort." (84)

"Oh royal one, all the way here we feared for our lives. Birds and beasts tormented us, as did the ill-omened owls, the *sang saek, thut, khut,* and *khao.* We take refuge in your merit, royal lord; may we be relieved of our fear." (85)

> The venerable one laughed and smiling broadly said,
> "I assure you, ladies, you have no cause to fear." (86)

"Return while you still see the sun and so make a timely exit from the forest. Hurry, and say to the princesses, 'I am going to help you now. Do not be troubled.'" (87)

Without delay, Roy and Ruen saluted him, taking leave with gladdened hearts, and together with the practitioner they returned to mount their elephants. Skirting along the edge of the foothills they made their way back along the trail. All the while they turned to look about them, now seeing unblemished trees, each like a beautiful palace, a celestial abode, a royal home, resplendent with an abundance of red flowers, shimmering like the royal ruby, and fresh green foliage shining like lustrous jade. Yellow blossoms shone like pure gold; white blossoms gleamed like countless pearls. The many species shone radiantly in the various habitats, with abundant beauty to capture the heart. They gradually descended to the lands below and admired there the many trees, pleasing to the lingering eye. And pleasing to the attending ear were the countless birds flocked together to call out their songs, resounding throughout the vast woodlands and forests. (88)

They heard the calls of parrots and mynas, the *sattawa* and flocks of koel. Cockatoos mixed with black-necked mynas. Thai mynas called out in pairs. Drongos called out, and striped barbets. The *khokma*[88] turned bashfully to the terns. Herons called out joyfully in their desire, and magpie robins spread their fans. There were swallows, ospreys, warblers, and coucals. Peacocks raised their feathers, dancing in display, gracefully swaying their tapering tails while peahens arrayed themselves about in attendance. Golden deer gathered together, side by side, and bow deer[89] sought bashfully for their mates. All were scattered about in profusion in countless flocks and herds, beautiful and pleasing to the eye. Tortoises and turtles wandered about the hidden places amid countless varieties of crab and fish. Waterfowl[90] were abundant everywhere. Swans glided through the air to their bathing pools. Ducks bobbed along the watercourses. Pelicans perambulated. Multitudes of *chakphrak*[91] stirred the water into foam. The cotton teals attended their mates as they swam. The lotus birds alighted on the lotus flowers. The bees bathed in intoxication amid the fine particles of pollen. Abundant lotus buds blossomed. The beautiful red lotus concealed the spreading petals of the white lotus, and the white lotus gave off fragrant lotus perfume. The blue lotus and red lotus overlapped in all their many varieties. The once terrifying jungle had become a place of contentment, gladness, pleasure, and joy. They urged the elephants along in haste, and when they had reached the palace of the princesses, standing nearby the palace of the king, they called the souls of the royal daughters. "Oh, souls of these two, come dwell within them, and be joined with their bodies. May the heat of fire not burn them. May fever never touch them. (89)[92]

> "Whatever they wish or want, may it not be denied them.
> May all come to pass as they desire. Be close to them, not separated
> even for a moment." (90)

As for the two daughters, they had set up a golden couch and stool with a canopy stretched above. And there they brought pillows and cushions of the greatest beauty, and curtains with dazzling embroidery. They sought out all manner of perfumed things and every type of fragrant flower. In place of puffed rice, they prepared precious gems and brought clusters of flowers wrought of silver and gold, all types of foods and things to eat, and varieties of wines and rice. All of this, which they had claimed was for the soul calling, they prepared as offerings to receive the venerable lord. (91)

And then suddenly
the venerable lord arrived, even before Phra Phuean and Phra
   Phaeng had reached the dwelling. (92)

The firmament darkened and dimmed as heavy clouds filled the heavens. In awed wonder the princesses brought their hands together in salute crying, "Perhaps our venerable lord is coming!" (93)

Casting about for their ladies-in-waiting
they spied them in the distance and felt as though they had gained
   possession of a kingdom. (94)

Preparing to sit in attendance,
the ladies-in-waiting dismounted the elephants and came to bow
   before the princesses. (95)

They looked about while paying their respects and asked,
"Does all of this foretell the coming of our venerable lord?" (96)

[Phuean and Phaeng] said, "It must be the exalted one.

The venerable one has come. There can be no doubt. (97)

"Come, we shall invoke the venerable lord."
Their hands joined above their heads, all bowed in obeisance. (98)

All about them they scattered puffed rice and flowers.
Offering incense, candles of gold, and words of praise, they bowed
    in salutation. (99)

"Lord of splendor surpassing the heavens,
we beg that you have pity on us. Please, make yourself visible
    to us." (100)

Attentively they saluted and invoked their protecting spirit:
"We ask that you show forth your power and not remain obscured
    from us.
We ask that you be an everlasting refuge for us.
We ask that you manifest yourself in bodily form, oh lord." (101)

Thereupon, the venerable one allowed them to see his presence,
Striking in form and stunning in shape, comely and strong.
Neither stout nor lean, but beautiful. Not young,
not old. Hair, skin, complexion, mouth, eyebrows, and eyes:
    lovely. (102)

The two princesses saw the venerable lord and they admired him.
They prostrated themselves, their arms in respectful salute.
They presented their many oblations,
carefully prepared for veneration. "Venerable lord, please accept
    these offerings." (103)

The venerable one saw the princesses' great respect.

His heart was moved with pity for them.

He accepted the offerings, so carefully made and respectfully
presented.

Seeing him receive the offerings, the princesses were greatly
pleased. (104)

And then they prostrated in worshipful salute,

relating their trouble in all its detail.

"Lord father, lift our troubled hearts.

When we find relief, we will tend to your every wish. (105)

"We shall present to you the nine gems and vast amounts of silver
and gold,

a wagon load of each, drawn up before you.

Pure white cattle and buffalo, with horns of gold, and swans, and
geese, and swine,

ducks and chickens, rice and wine, all will we present to you in
gratitude." (106)

The venerable one listened but he replied, "Oh, how shameful!

Offer me no bribes, for I despise such things!

Loyal respect is the only thing of surpassing value.

This malady will depart from you. Let not your hearts be troubled.
(107)

"I am not some hapless ghost with severed intestines, come here in
hungry distress,

roving about, wandering in constant search

and telling lies and falsehoods to those who present offerings.

It is a shameful wrong to fill the stomach by despicable deeds. (108)

"I am the divine lord of the great mountains,
known to all by the title 'venerable lord.'
The power of my merit increases without end.
I have ruled the earth for a million years and will do so until the end
of time.[93] (109)

"Splendid power and authority are mine, by virtue of my good
deeds,
accrued as a fund of merit against all distress.
Treasures of great value flood in upon me
from all the world, one upon the other, surpassing in perfection.
(110)

"I see you and I am moved to great compassion.
I will help you, princesses—be not distressed.
I will invite Phra Lo to come to you.
Do not be in such pain, but wait for news." (111)

The two acknowledged him, and prostrating they asked,
"How much longer will it be before the beautiful ruler will come?"
The venerable one replied to them, "This is no base or ordinary
man, good ladies,
but an exalted ruler, son of a reigning lord, a man of merit. (112)

"They have many seasoned practitioners to counter my magic.
It is not possible to specify the time as you ask me to do.
Please try to be patient. He will not escape us.
Before too long the king will come to us. (113)

"So be still and wait.

Should you see that the king is slow in coming, have someone go to
remind me." (114)

Instructing the two to wash their precious hair,[94]
and wishing them success, the venerable lord took leave of them.
(115)

They fixed their eyes upon him as he departed.
In an instant he vanished from sight, swift as the blowing breeze.
(116)

Speeding swiftly to his abode, the venerable one took vines and
bamboo and with them plaited a wind charm.[95] In its center he drew
the king, with one of the princesses on each side, bent in supplication,
embracing him and enticing him to come. And he arrayed magical
symbols all about the four edges. He whispered quiet chants and
turning saw a *yang* tree seven spans in girth. With clenched fist, he
struck the tree to bend it over, and its tip lowered to the ground. (117)

As the tree took in the words of the venerable one, Phra Lo felt a
strange sensation stir his heart. The venerable one fastened the device
to the treetop then placed his hand upon it for a moment, and the
treetop began to lift. The leaves fluttered about, and then the tree
sprang suddenly upright. The breezes blew, spinning the device like
a pinwheel suspended on high. And King Lo, too, spun: "Whoosh!"
The wind spun him round. (118)

In a dream, Phra Lo saw the royal Phuean and golden Phaeng,
the two lying close, pressing in on either side of him,

73

the two, arms entwined, embracing him.
Unceasingly they called to him to come to the city of Song. (119)

The lord awoke from his sleep,
and in melancholy depression, in lonely longing, he sighed. (120)

The king did not regain his good disposition. The royal concubines took note and drew each other's attention to his affliction. And then they took this strange news to the queen mother. When she had heard them out, her heart was consumed by fire. She went to her child and saw the strange situation. Saying, "My beloved child, what has brought you to this, so painful for me to see?" The king replied, "Today my body is shaken, and my heart buffeted by disquiet. In a dream, I saw most clearly the two princesses, the golden Phuean and Phaeng, lying close on either side of me, our faces pressed together in embrace. They entwined me in their arms, embracing me in supplication, and with soothing caresses invited me to go to them. My heart raced as though near collapse. My breast spun as though to overturn. My suffering is boundless, my sadness beyond measure! I yearn to go in search of them, and if I should take leave of you, oh mother, I beg of you, have pity on me, your son." (121)

The queen listened as her child told his story,
her heart consumed with flames of love.
Her tears became a stream, pouring down in profusion.
Sobbing countless sobs, she cried out in suffering. (122)

She struck her breast, "Oh child, beloved son,
how did you come to this?
All the treasures that fill our kingdom,

countless and beyond measure, I will use to care for you. (123)

"Kaew![96] Do not delay! Mount a search!
Bring the royal astrologers, quickly!
Bring the chief physicians and the spirit practitioners!
Bring every sorceress and all who can repel magic! (124)

"Khwan! Go! Summon everyone!
Bring every lord and noble, every retainer, to come and help.
Let those who know the wilderness scour the forests for every sort
      of curative,
and from our storehouses collect all the remedies brought from near
      and far.[97] (125)

"My stores and those of my child,
I will use all in caring for him.

Even if I should use up everything in our realm,
I use up only things. May he regain his strength!" (126)

They searched until all was as it ought to be.
Whatever the practitioners called for, it was done.
Before long Phra Lo found relief and was again radiant and
      comfortable.
The queen rewarded each of the practitioners extravagantly. (127)

The queen, too, regained her strength of heart and
the concubines their freshness of face.
From the royal councilors to the common peasants, all were relieved
      and made well.

The king brightened, and the delirium left him. (128)

But the two princesses remained, waiting
for news of Phra Lo, slow in coming. Their breasts were hot as
fire. (129)

They sent a reminder to the venerable lord,
who said, "They must have seasoned practitioners, skilled at
undoing our magic spells." (130)

He took a flag of victory[98] arrayed with more magic symbols than
he'd used before. And on it he drew the king seated in the center
with the princesses at his sides, tightly embracing and pulling him to
them. And then he passed his hands over a great ironwood tree, no
ordinary tree but one nine spans in size, and blew upon it with his
breath. The treetop bent down before him, and to it he affixed the flag
and then pushed it back up. At first the tree trunk shook, and then the
leaves fluttered and slapped together. Then the tree trunk abruptly
straightened itself and stood upright. The breeze buffeted the flag,
snapping it about. The winds pushed at the flag and the breezes pulled
at it, swiftly spreading its potions. And they touched the king. He felt
as if the princesses themselves had appeared before him, stroking
and caressing him. (131)

The lord was more powerfully moved than before, as if he were seeing
the princesses with his own eyes, come to invite him to their dwelling,
enticing him to their abode. His heart trembled in distress, his body
shaken by a deep chill, and he turned his face to the direction of the
rising sun.[99] All this was reported to Lady Bunluea, who rushed in
a frenzy to her son. She came, crying and disheartened, and sank

down sadly gazing at Phra Lo. She struck her breast and cried, "Oh, my precious child. (132)

> "Your fever was a torment to me, like the weight of a mountain.
> As your suffering lessened, so did my own distress.
> Now I come and see you more troubled than before.
> Torment is piled upon torment, heavier than the weight of all the
>   skies. (133)

> "There is no one in this land who understands our difficulty.
> They will see only the two of us, partners in death.
> How so ever did we come to this?
> If you should die, my son, I will die with you. (134)

> "Khwan! Kaew! Renew and intensify your searches.
> Bring all the practitioners, every last one.
> Hasten them here to tend to the love of my life.
> Hurry! There is no time to waste! Help us, with every fiber of your
>   being." (135)

> They located every group and kind of practitioner
> throughout the kingdom, omitting no one.
> All came to minister to Phra Lo, but he experienced no change.
> The queen mother was perplexed. (136)

> Her majesty summoned all her ministers.
> Opening the curtain[100] to speak she said,
> "His highness, our sovereign king,
> has not been relieved of his fever. A raging love is lodged within his
>   heart. (137)

"Examine again the groups of practitioners. Look to every one of
  them.
See if anyone has been overlooked.
Consider anything that might be helpful.
Quickly! Try anything that might be of use." (138)

The ministers followed the royal order. They considered every one
of the practitioners and so came to realize that the one known as
Sitthichai,[101] who had gone to be in the forest, knew more of esoteric
spells and arcane potions than any of the many other practitioners.
He had delved deeply into the arts of enchantment, acquiring vast
power. The most skillful practitioner of magic, he was imbued with
supernatural powers. Lady Bunluea gave the order and so they
hastened to bring this venerable one to her. He then performed a fire
ceremony, offering sacrifice to powerful divinities. He chanted sacred
magic incantations, conjoined in accordance with the formulas, to
bring Phra Lo out of his confusion, and he bade the lord bathe in
lustral water. Then the universal lord, brighter and happier, consumed
these remedies of great efficacy, endowed with special supernatural
power, and cleansed his royal hair and body. Sitthichai then built a
mandala of three tiers, and in the inner portion he placed guardian
spirits, and in the middle, protective giants, and at the outer door
he placed demons. In the surrounding air, he stationed legions of
ghosts to keep watch all about them. He then prepared a grand ritual,
a ceremony of celebration and a *baisi*[102] to call the soul of the king.
And so the king rewarded them, bestowing a grand array of valuable
possessions upon the practitioner Sitthichai as well as upon the other
practitioners, each according to his due. And he presented also sets of
garments to each one who had attended and ministered to him. (139)

THE STORY OF KING LO

Oh, pity the two princesses!

They waited but did not see him, their breasts enflamed with
longing.

"Is Phra Lo to come or is he not?"

They wept and moaned, waiting only for the king. (140)

And so they sent their ladies-in-waiting

to ask the venerable one what had come to pass.

[Ruen and Roy] went to pay their respects to him, saying

"Oh royal venerable one, how much longer will it be before the lord
comes?" (141)

[Samingphrai replied,] "I have used my powers to view all things."

He said that they had countered his magic and were now on guard.

"It is most difficult to outdo their practitioners, but

leave this to me. I shall contend with them myself." (142)

"Be not alarmed by the delay.

The princesses will soon see his face. The king will soon come to
them." (143)

The venerable one contemplated and then called forth powerful
spirits from the forest, from the waters and the banks, from the
caverns and the caves. From every direction, from every locality they
came to attend the venerable one. The most powerful in the entourage
organized the spirits about him, and for the divinities and the giants
he appointed leaders. So a vast retinue of spirits and demons formed
about him, boundless in numbers, and directed by a commander for
every group. Bold, audacious spirits with great powers he appointed
as officers and officials. The chieftains he bade ride upon elephants.[103]

Some rode tigers and lions. Some rode bears and boars. Some rode snakes and serpents. Some rode albino horses, and cattle, and buffalo, and rhinoceros. Each bellowed out its call, echoing fearfully. The spirits transformed themselves into many strange shapes. They became as birds of the raven family, with heads of crows and vultures. They conjured up heads of tigers and panthers, deer and stags, with strange and diverse bodies. Crowding together they took up arms, excellent implements of war. They leaped up and ran about, calling out loudly, threatening with boisterous sounds. They tore up trees and rocks and stones, and massing together in a speeding horde they roared out with a thunderous echo, the sound shaking the very earth. When the spectral force was assembled and arrayed, the venerable one laid out the orders in detail and so specified the strategy that they would use. Giving them both potions and incantations, he detailed the tactics they would employ. He gave magic potions to render the opposition weak and formulas to dissipate their power, to make their protecting spirits flee. "Once their spirits are conquered I will use the *sala hoen*[104] to entice the king to come to the dwelling of the princesses. Do not deviate from the orders I here give." (144)

Awesome were forces of the lord of the great mountains.
With uproar filling the heavens they set out,
the mountain spirits and the assemblage of ghosts abundant beyond
counting.
They pressed forward urgently, spreading throughout all the sky.
(145)

This ghostly horde resembled the forces of the great demon Mara,
filling the forests and the woods, crushing all before them.

Before long they arrived at their destination, the territory of the
    king.
The spirits of that territory urgently called out to one another. (146)

They joined in great numbers to defend their territory. The invading
spirits attacked threateningly, and the defending spirits pushed
forward, hurling themselves into the fight. They rushed about,
leaping, chasing and harassing the invaders. But some slipped away,
fled, or hid themselves without returning the blows. (147)

[In confusion the attackers and the defenders fought.
Ghosts beat down ghosts, chasing and stabbing, dodging and
    feinting—
twisting and turning, shouting out loudly, urging on the troops.
The invaders attacked fiercely, fighting, slashing, and destroying.]
    (148)[105]

In confusion they fought, in thundering, powerful combat. Ghosts
threw down ghosts, chasing and stabbing. Fighting fiercely, shouting,
feinting, the ghosts loyal to the lord were fierce. Shouting out to urge
on their defense, they joined together to carry on the fight. (149)

The ghosts created an inferno causing smoke to obscure the heavens.
The potions and incantations of the attackers were filled with power,
and the local spirits had great difficulty resisting. So they entrusted
the news to the winds, booming boisterously throughout the sky.
The winds came swiftly and informed the divinities, guardian spirits
of the city, "The heavens and the earth are yellowed with omens of
calamity. The air is befouled with billows of smoke, and the skies are
shaken with bolts of thunder. The heart of the city is overwhelmed

and near collapse." The divinities listened in consternation, stunned, shaking and quivering with fear of the might and enormous power of the royal venerable one. The practitioner Sitthichai used his power to see. "A great misfortune has come upon us," he said. This venerable practitioner contemplated these things. "My teacher explained such things to me, and I see clearly what has come about. All this was brought about by the power and might of a formidable spirit." And so he revealed this to the queen mother, who learned to her astonishment that there was no defense. Seeing this strange misfortune, she fell into lamentation. She beat her breast and cried, "Who can save our lord, my son, my great love? (150)

"Venerable practitioner, how has this come about? Oh, alas!
Please, use your power to examine this for me.
Oh, have pity on us. Please help us.
Deliver us, and I will give you half of my city!" (151)

The venerable one contemplated and then said, "My lady, this is
    much beyond me.
They are aided by a divinity of great power and might.
Our spirits and guardian divinities are vanquished and have fled.
A great one's wiles have overwhelmed our own. (152)

"Everything that we have has been used in the defense.
All our divinities, all our spirits have fled before the victors.
All our potions and remedies are rendered powerless.
Our incantations and medications cannot withstand this excellent
    one." (153)

Oh pitiable lady, queen and mother.

She listened, consumed by the heat of inestimable sadness.
Her tears were as a stream in flood, flowing down.
She sobbed out countless sobs, until her heart was parched and
    dry. (154)

The inner spirits rushed out, and the outer spirits rushed in. The divinities sent by the venerable lord came and did as he had taught them, causing weakness and dismay everywhere. Reports were carried back, and the news reached Samingphrai. The venerable lord listened and then he caused the *sala hoen* to pass through the sky and fall to rest, mixed in among the betel nut of the king. King Lo picked up and took the potion, and in no time he felt his heart weaken. Of the beautiful sisters he thought, "I don't know what to do," and he was filled with dark dismay. (155)

The lord informed his noble queen mother,
"I salute at your feet, exalted one.
Oh, I live with a heavy heart.
I wish to take leave of you, mother, to travel about the forests." (156)

The queen heard her noble son take his leave of her.
"My beloved, however came you to be this way?
Our spirit practitioners, who cared for and preserved you,
have reached the limits of their power. They have told of the great
    difficulties. (157)

"Even more spirits have been sent here against us,
and more trickery and deceptions and potions.
On the day that you set out to take leave of me,
fever will wither my breast, and I will be brought down." (158)

Phra Lo could not leave, and remained enduring his suffering,
now sitting, now lying, arising and sighing.
Kingship brought him no peace. He ruled in great sadness.
He longed for the charming princesses and found no comfort. (159)

The queen pressed close, attending the great monarch,
caring for his highness, her king.
The royal concubines waved fans, swinging them back and forth,
    fanning him.
The royal queen mother caressed him, consoling his spirit. (160)

Phra Lo found no release from his sadness; his soul remained
    troubled.
In his sleep, he cried out deliriously for the princesses.
His heart was oppressed with fear that his desire would be
    unfulfilled.
He thought, "Alas! I wish I were dead." (161)

On arising he implored, "I wish to go,
to enjoy the woods and to hunt the elephant,
to enjoy the mountainous forests and hunt there for game,
to enjoy the deep untamed jungles and the caves and the great
    lakes." (162)

The queen listened to her son with deep concern.
"He says he is going to admire the flowers.
But once he has left, he will go to unite with the princesses.
It is a deception, but how can I refuse his incessant pleading?" (163)

She summoned the astrologers and all the most respected ministers.

She summoned venerable Sitthichai to come to her
and informed them of all things.
The astrologers said, "How can one control the ruler of a
kingdom?" (164)

Sitthichai said to the queen,
"Even divinities could not restrain him."
The ministers said, "Nothing can prevail over him.
Let us send messengers to seek knowledge of these happenings." (165)

She thanked her ministers for their counsel:
"What you suggest is truly good.
No other solutions have prevailed,
and so this should be done." (166)

Then she herself went
to say to Phra Lo, "My dear one, take pity on your mother." (167)

"I have listened to you tell me that you wish to seek sport in the forest
and to admire the mountains. But I can guess that this is not the real
meaning of your words. You have something else in mind. Speak
truthfully to me, so that I may know fully." (168)

[Phra Lo replied,] "I indeed have other intentions.
If I should tell them to you, you must not hinder me." (169)

[Bunluea replied,] "In whatever has pleased you, precious one,
have I ever yet deprived you or opposed your wishes? (170)

"It shall be as you like,

all in accord with your wishes. I will not resist you in your
distress." (171)

[Phra Lo replied,] "Oh my beloved queen, I
wish to go to see the faces of the noble Phuean and golden
Phaeng." (172)

"I have not attained my goal
and cannot surrender my desire for them, oh my mother." (173)

"I take leave of you, my queen.
I will go to the two of them, and then I will return." (174)

[Bunluea replied,] "If you do go, how will you return, oh my lord,
my child?
If prey went in search of the tiger, would the tiger spare its life?
Listening to your words, I do not know what to think.
I cannot think, and I am only burning with discomfort. (175)

"We must do what is fitting.
An emissary will be sent to ask for the two sisters.
We will receive them to be with you.
This can be easily done, without even the thread of a spider's web as
hindrance." (176)

[Phra Lo replied,] "Your plan, my queen, would take too long,
and perhaps their father would not agree.
The way is far, and carrying messages back and forth would be
difficult.
It would be easier in every way if I went myself." (177)

[Lady Bunluea replied,] "Once you are gone, my lord, can you return
    in safety?

You will not escape, oh king. Do not go!

Their potions and incantations are exceedingly powerful.

The specters are fierce. The people are fierce. How will you escape in
    safety? (178)

"Our city has seen terrible omens, my child.

They have sent powerful spirits to oppress us.

Can you, young man, pinnacle of the three realms, avoid

the collapse of the kingdom, your own collapse, the loss of your
    sovereignty?" (179)

Then the queen told this story to Phra Lo:

"We attacked their grandfather and severed his head.

They bear hatred for us and hope to avenge themselves.

And are you going to walk into their clutches?" (180)

[Phra Lo responded,] "When my fate calls me, how can I resist?

If it is not my fate, then who can kill me?

If it is merit that motivates me, I will reach a place of happiness.

If my motivation is misdeeds, I will be brought low, and how can I
    be helped? (181)

"If in going there I am to meet my end,

descending into a hell of endless suffering and scorching flames, so
    be it.

Or if in staying here I were to ascend into a heaven of the greatest
    joys, so be it.

Still, I will not remain. So, I take leave of you and I will go." (182)

She struck her breast and cried out as though approaching death,
"I have taught you all I know. I can teach you no more.
Perhaps it is your karma that is ensnaring you.
Despite your knowledge, you cannot restrain yourself, caught up in
    intoxicating madness. (183)

"I observed faithfully all the prescribed practices of the seven days,
    oh son.
I opened the storehouses to share our bounty in measure great as
    the sky,
asking for a fair-minded child, a son pleasing to my heart.
And so, I conceived you, my ruler, my greatest joy. (184)

"For ten months, I carried you.[106]
I cared for you myself, ever attentive.
When you deigned to be born,
I nurtured you, bathing and holding you, caressing and feeding and
    caring for you. (185)

"Each day I myself fed you your three meals,
never letting anyone wrong you.
I nurtured you ceaselessly and was never displeased with you,
caring for you until the time that you could feed yourself. (186)

"I carefully prepared your food and arranged your meals.
Constant always, never forgetting even a bit.
I oversaw and arranged all your meals myself,
never relaxing the least bit or allowing others to see to the task." (187)

"From the very first I nourished and cared for you

as you came of age until you obtained
all the treasures of the sovereignty, reigning as king.
And now can you insist on departing, leaving your mother in
    desolation? (188)

"I have lived my life hoping to depend on you
and intending, at my death, to entrust my remains to you.
How can you now depart from me?
And when I die, who shall I trust to cremate my remains? (189)

"With all my heart I have forbidden you.
I have reasoned with you, but you have not listened and yet will go.
My heart is heavy, stricken with terrible suffering.
I remain behind, comfortless, with only sadness and great
    sorrow. (190)

"My child, you are leaving me. Oh, what karma is it
that makes you so determined to go to those pretty ones?
I will be alone, to suffer in misery.
Come. Let me look upon you and so lessen my sorrow." (191)

She admired his cheeks, his forehead, and his hairline.
She admired his mouth and his beautifully radiant eyes.
She admired his face, like the shining moon, beguiling to the eye.
The excellent one was lovely. She kissed his cheek and caressed
    his ear. (192)

She kissed his nose. What scent could compare?
She kissed his chin, his throat, and she was overcome.
She kissed his flesh, his flawless breast.

"I kiss your shoulder, back, chest, and do so again. I kiss your sides
and caress your arms." (193)

She wished to admire all his body.
But he raised his hands in salute and said,
"You ought to kiss only the crown of my head.
Kiss my cheeks and hair, oh royal lady, should you wish, to bid me
farewell." (194)

"Oh, my precious darling child. Pity me!
I would rest your feet upon my head.
Why do you resist me?
I would kiss your feet to bid you farewell" (195)

[Phra Lo answered,] "You love me, and yet would place me above
your head?
I fear this would be a grievous wrong.
You gave me the gift of life and guided me as I grew.
I cannot repay your kindness, not even so much as the strand of a
spider's web. (196)

"Perhaps it is karma that takes me from you, my queen.
Perhaps it is the misdeeds of the past that force me to leave you.
Your kindness is unrequited, your heart's desires are unfulfilled,
because their potions have drawn me into this great confusion." (197)

And then the beautiful queen mother moaned, her heart a melancholy
void.[107] "Peerless Lord Lo, I love you more than my eyes or body, more
than my life or my existence. Now you are to leave me, forsaking your
mother, forsaking your royal city. A great ruler has seven attributes

that you must remember.[108] Memorize these words of your mother and do not abandon them. Do not neglect the rites of the noble born. Do not be negligent, forgetting yourself. Do not associate with untruthful people. Consider carefully and only then act. Weigh each word and only then speak. Do not bring difficulties upon your subjects. Judge all matters of state straightforwardly. Govern your kingdom so that all will have comfort. Eliminate all distress both internal and external. Concern yourself with every department. Do not be attracted to falsehood. Deliberate, and then follow the way of justice. What you would prevent, prevent completely. What you would suppress, suppress artfully. Examine both your guides and your servants. Select only the trustworthy. Choose your counselors with care. Instill boldness in your people. Destroy the parasites who weaken your realm. Punish subjects who violate our laws. Deter those who dare to aid our enemies. Suppress wickedness so it cannot arise. Do not seek ripeness before its time. Do not tether a horse from both sides. Do not drag poison behind you. Do not cause people to hate and secretly curse you. Conduct yourself so that others will love you. Persuade others to seek after the heavens. In the future, the divinities will praise you, so you must do what is right. Do not neglect contemplation. Be unhurried in your deliberations so that your dignity will not be lost. When the skies and the earth and the heavens come to their end, may the consuming conflagration not destroy you. Follow these instructions of your mother. Oh, your mother's greatest love, may you prosper. (198)

"May you prosper in honor and in the fullness of power.

May you not know suffering, sadness, illness, or misfortune.

May enemies and forces of evil flee before your might.

May you be happy and know neither anger nor vengefulness. (199)[109]

"May you achieve union as you wish with the two beautiful ladies.
May you not fall prey to wiles of the heart.
May you be mindful and not grow weary of my instruction.
May you, dear one, hasten to return to protect the territory of your
  great city. (200)

"I entrust my child to all the divinities, guardians of the earth,
of the air, of the trees, of the waters, and of the vast jungles.
Shiva, Vishnu, Indra, and Brahma,
help to protect the elephant lord. Keep him from danger. (201)

"Return this great monarch to me alive.
I shall prepare banners and flags and umbrellas of shining beauty,
golden candles festooned with gems, beautiful and refreshing to the
  eye,
ducks and chickens and *baisi* to be placed everywhere in
  repayment." (202)

The lord heard the words of the queen
and bowed low in respectful prostration, accepting her words of
  instruction. (203)

He received her blessings, showered down upon his head.
He undid his hair and with it wiped his mother's feet. (204)

He raised his hands above his head in salute.
Taking leave of her, he entered the audience hall. (205)

He gave his orders to the counselors, his own loyal assistants. "Remain
here on watch in my stead and carry on with governing. You must

care for our dominion. Watch over my subjects and keep them from wrath. Deal swiftly with enemies. And protect my queen as I always have." (206)

And then he spoke his orders to the commanders of his forces, stalwart men, ferocious and bold. "Hasten to prepare a marching formation of the four divisions,[110] resplendent in arms, replete in every group and section. See to it that everything is in order and that all is in accord with discipline. Prepare immediately! I shall embark upon my journey tomorrow at the dawning of the day." (207)

He then proceeded to the chambers
of the royal residence, there to comfort and take leave of his wife.
  "Be well, dear lady. (208)

"I am to make my way.
Stay, dear one, stay and do not be sad. Before long I shall return to
  unite with you." (209)

Sorrow filled the breast of Laksanawadi
with sadness that nearly turned her tears to blood; her eyes swelled,
  a wellspring of tears. (210)

With hands raised in respectful salute, she addressed the lord of the
  earth,
"Royal one, are you to leave me here in solitude? (211)

"The way is long, and you may encounter ferocious animals.
Fearsome ghosts may try to intimidate you, by trickery appearing
  before your eyes." (212)

"I fear the enemies that lie before you, and
for me, left here behind, if you were to die I would feel blinded. (213)

"I beg to forbid you to leave, my lord.
Remain here as my protector. Oh, I beseech you not to go! (214)[111]

"I left behind my father, my mother, all of my family.
You deigned to bring me here to raise and provide for me.
As your spouse I have found great happiness.
Your departure will be as though my head were severed." (214a)[112]

[Phra Lo replied,] "All things of this earth are transitory.
Only one's deeds, both the evil and the meritorious, are truly lasting.
As a shadow follows the body, so do they cling to us.
In accordance with our merit and evil we find succor and aid. (215)

"Although I leave you, my beloved, my heart is sorely distressed.
I leave one union to find another, and fear that I may not succeed.
But if I were to stay my breast would be crushed by love.
I must leave you behind, but soon I will return to reunite with you."
    (216)

[Laksanawadi replied,] "If you do go and unite with them,
how so ever will you return to be my protector?
Have no hope that this will come about. They will not release you to
    return.
They will seduce you and trap you there in solitude." (217)

[Phra Lo answered,] "I must go. I must leave you, my beloved.
Their incantations and potions force me to set forth and go.

If I were to stay, dear wife, there would be no joy in our
   togetherness.
If death did not take me from you I would be driven to insanity."
   (218a)[113]

[Laksanawadi replied,] "From my youth, when I knew nothing and
   had yet to come of age,
you took me to nourish and to care for.
You were the pinnacle of my life. You were my mother,
my father, and my lord. Day and night, you were my teacher."
   (218b)[114]

She placed her head in his lap.
Her arms tightly embraced him.
With every breath she kissed him, but she found no satisfaction.
And she anointed her head with dust from the sole of his foot. (219)

Seeing sorrow piled upon sorrow, the king joined his lady in
   sadness.
He caressed her and he calmed her.
"Be not sorrowful. It is a bad omen for my going into the wooded
   forests.
Rid yourself of suffering and of enmity, for vexation will rob you of
   your beauty." (220)

When he had finished with his comforting, he instructed his
   concubines.
"Ladies, do not be overwhelmed by the fires of grief."
The company of ladies received the orders from their exalted
   husband.

They hung their heads and sobbed, crying out loudly in unison. (221)

The sound of crying and wailing pervaded the royal residence.
All the officials and the counselors were sickened with agitation.
In their homes, all the populace repeatedly struck their breasts in
    suffering.
The city was cooled by the flowing water of tears of desolation. (222)

Seeing everyone in tears, both men and women,
the king was shaken and disheartened.
"Oh be not consumed by unbounded sadness.
Great suffering will bring on fever, illness that may lead to death." (223)

Grief gradually faded from his heart, and he gave instructions to
his queen and all his concubines. The lord had not yet slept when
the moon and the many stars slipped away, fading slowly before the
dawn. The morning star pierced the sky, and the rooster opened its
eyes and beat its wings, crying out with vigor, while the koel called
out its warning. He made his way to his toilet, and the water ladies
performed their duties. He then proceeded to his bath, and quickly he
was cleansed. He was sprinkled with fragrant powders and perfumes
and fragrances mixed with gold. Carefully he was dressed in excellent
leggings, elegantly patterned garments, and a sash, all of them radiant
with beauty. He looked upon the decorative sash, gracefully swaying
and flowing like a vine.[115] Clothing and garments of various colors
were bound, shimmering, about his breast. Double chains were strung
together with a golden neckpiece. His breastplate gave off a lustrous
gleam, diamonds and gems glittering with comeliness. He put on
his shining bracelets, *mangkon*-shaped armlets,[116] dazzling, sparkling
finger rings, and a precious crown of polished beauty. Having taken

up his victory weapons he made his way, stepping as serenely as the exalted lion king striding from its gem-strewn cave. He arrived at the royal platform, and quickly his expert mahout drove the elephant to the mounting spot. Having ascended the neck of the majestic tusker, he bade his forces set out. (224)

Horns, conchs, and orchestras of gongs
sounded a festive fanfare, resounding throughout his entire city. (225)

The elephant Phaya Chainuphap[117] trumpeted loudly, echoing
through the forest.
Greatly aroused, he tossed his head and bellowed.
Most beautiful in every way, he held a place in the king's heart.
His festoons and head cloths shimmered like diamonds, lustrous as
stars. (226)

The king took up the goad, magnificent in his dignity,
with the bearing of an immortal god come to earth.
Beautiful elephant and beautiful king, a great divinity could not
compare.
The praiseworthy forces were all like divinities descended from the
heavens to the earth. (227)

The forward flags set out, leading the forces. They waved on high, giving signals to move the many troops in each formation. The supervisors and inspectors arranged all in proper order, coming forward in ranks and files, expanding the intervals as appropriate. The officers carried lances, held at the ready, red tassels fluttering in the breeze, and across their chests hung great bows and arrows. The glorious decorations of the horses, beautifully turned out, shimmered with bright gems and gold. The Sindhu steeds,[118] surpassing all in appearance, pranced and reared, headstrong and eager. In fighting the enemy such mounts bring victory. Officials, each of royal rank, powerfully compelled their mounts forward. Many were the mounted lords, and numerous were the mounted nobles of *muen* rank. Many were the horsemen[119] and their officers, all shimmering and radiant. With much ostentation, all their vast number followed after the king. Those moving to the fore were many; those bringing up the rear were numerous. On the left, they went in abundance; on the right, they went in great numbers, diverse and beautiful in every respect. In formations beyond counting they went, mounted on magnificent steeds of the finest markings, the most beautiful and graceful in the land. See them, each more beautiful than the next, surpassing even those of the heavenly realms. (228)

Look upon the magnificent troops. Bright flags fluttered, directing them, arranged in companies one hundred and one thousand strong and with companies of reserves and skirmishers. In procession they surrounded the lords and nobles in a great boisterous mass, numerous beyond counting. See the cohorts of shield bearers and of swordsmen, and archers with arrows bathed in poison. See the valiant spearmen. See the magnificent halberdiers. The forearm shield carriers followed the body shield carriers and the lance men and the many with fire hurlers. Oh, valiant forces, radiant, beautiful, magnificent![120] The commoners walked and their officers walked, directing them. Resolute officers rode the tall elephants, daring and bold, their neckpieces decorated with the magnificent *garuda*.[121] They marched in great formations, with swordsmen deployed to the left and to the right, to the front and to the rear, and at each foot of the royal pachyderm. Guarding over the king in their positions were swordsmen at the elephant's feet, encircling and protecting the royal mount. Swordsmen of the king's bodyguard press in tightly, surrounding the elephant, driving the two-tusked bearer of the jeweled throne. This courageous multitude accompanied the king's progress, bearing the most precious of royal adornments, the most excellent of decorations, the adornments of this, the most regal of kings. (229)

See the tiered parasols shimmer colorfully, blocking from view the tiered umbrellas, colorfully brilliant. Sheaves of festive peacock feathers and parasols were splendid before the eyes of the world, with the royal fan, the regal hair switch—all the regalia of the king. On both sides were the brightly shining regal insignia, carried by his retinue. Foods and utensils followed behind the golden palanquin throne, in countless groups directed by numerous officers, daring and bold. The marchers to the front abounded. The marchers to the rear were innumerable. Those on the left were beyond calculation; those on the right beyond estimation. Extending beyond both sides of the roadway they formed an expansive perimeter. With great festive call, the sound of conches and of horns and ensembles of gongs echoed forth, shaking the very earth as the great king set out with the masses of his troops, beyond magnificence. (230)[122]

The king was radiant as the moon.
He made his way as the lunar sphere passes through a cloudless sky.
The numerous stars, arrayed in their courses,
resemble his forces arrayed about him in procession. (231)

He gazed upon his subjects, their fences and homes, their gardens, orchards, and fields.

Looking upon their fields, he thinks of his loved one.

"By now you may be weeping over me, oh royal one,

afflicted at heart, moaning in pain, and who will console you?[123] (232)

"Going, I do not wish to leave my queen.

Wishing to return, I think of the princesses who await me.

It is good to go; it is not good to go—which of these?

Thoughts intensify my emptiness. Troubled by what may lie ahead,

    I yearn for what lies behind." (233)

Behind him lay happiness, imbued with love.

But before him, their potions were most powerful.

Return? Could the great Phra Lo have hoped to return?

He dismissed a return and determined to go on. (234)

The troops hurried along upon their journey, passing through farm and field, traversing many great roads. When they came to the outer reaches of the kingdom the guides announced the name of the district, and orders were given to halt the march and make camp. The troops set about erecting a dwelling, decorated in proper manner, and the king made his way to his royal pavilion, where the vast numbers of commanders sat awaiting their royal lord. (235)

The two attendants cared for their king, and his chamberlains took up their appointed tasks, attending to their duties in great numbers. The sun dropped low in the sky, and darkness steadily approached. The languid breezes stirred memories of his beloved, and he thought of his heavenly queen and pleasing companion, Laksanawadi, and of his lovely concubines. With his hands he stroked his breast, "Oh, I hastened to take leave of you, yet I am beset with grief. (236)

"I see the moon and it is like the face of my beloved.
I call to you, beautiful one, and I await you.
But I look again and see only the mark of the rabbit.[124]
The moon is cheerful, like a smiling face, yet I wish I could cease
    breathing and die. (237)

"I see the multitude of stars in the heavens above
like my many youthful concubines come to attend me.
Looking on them is surely to see the stars arrayed before me.
Oh, beautiful young concubines, deserted and loveless in your
    youth! (238)

"Sleeping alone, I ache in loneliness.
My arms wrapped around my breast, I sob, separated from love, far
    from my wife. (239)

"Seeing the forests and the flowers stirs and stimulates me.
Their lovely scent is like your fragrance, my lady, pervading the
    air." (240)

"The birds couple with their mates, feeding each other
just as you, young one, tease me with your whimpering, drawing me
    to caress you." (241)

"I think of your lovely form,
and it is as if I see your face, my heart's young delight." (242)

[To Kaew and Khwan he said,] "Why is it that you two, my
    attendants,
have not a single word to say? You should not be mute. (243)

"I beg you to help me laugh and so preserve my dignity.
I look upon these country folk, and I beg of you, look as well. (244)

"Their homes are not like those of our city.
Their dwellings are ugly hovels.
I see nothing here to interest the eye.
Seeing such things, I want to turn away and not even look." (245)

[Kaew and Khwan replied,] "Oh Lord, to cool the body one will
    bathe even in cloudy water,
and in time of hunger eat fermented fish[125] despite its rancid smell.
And when desire must be satisfied, lowborn women are sometimes
    a necessity.
Deprivation may weaken you, and how will you be able to live? (246)

"In times of want, one plucks the bloom of grass to decorate the hair
and admires its minimal fragrance, like one who has lost his senses.
So admire the scent of the *sukkrom* tree and the *lamduan* tree, oh
    royal one.
Admire the fragrance and let it satisfy, like the fragrance of your
    loved one." (247)

The two men engaged the king in conversation.
The royal one spoke with them, but his heart was with his love.
In part, he yearned for the two women, Phuean and Phaeng.
In part, he thought of his queen and his youthful royal
    concubines. (248)

The king, beautiful of form and noble of birth,
clasped his pillow in fevered isolation, passion burning his heart. (249)

A bright, clear moon lit the sky.
The excellent Lo, lord of the earth, set forth. (250)

The troops continued along in their journey, passing through fields of
rice and through fields of grass. The leaders pressed into the thickets
of *lao* grass and into thickets of *faek* grass, and thickets of *khaem*
grass intermixed with *kha* grass. They reached the leafy forests and
the jungle, where they saw the tall stately trees of the deep forests,
groves of trees, strong and thick. The king admired them, happily
pointing, "These trees, and those, by what names are they called?" (251)

The forest hunters knew them by heart,
and they told the king the names of each one. (252)

Once he had learned the names with certainty,
King Lo praised the precious trees: "They are like my precious loved
  ones. (253)

"The *aen khlao* tree is like my dear one, caressing and fondling
  me.[126]
Catching its fragrance, I am reminded of the fragrance of my lady.
The *sukkrom* and *phayom* trees please me,
like the fragrance of my queen. Enchanting! (254)

"The 'lady's smile' flower is like my dear lady's smile of happiness.
The 'touch' flower is like the touch of my angel's hand.
The 'lady's tresses' is the hair of my queen, flowing down, is it not?
The 'love' flower is my love for her, joining me in love. (255)

"The 'follow' tree is like my lady, who would follow me.

The waving of its leaves is as my queen, waving to beckon me.
I see the 'tress'[127] fruit tree and I pine for the tresses of my dear one.
The vines enfold the tree trunks as the gentle one encircles my
    waist. (256)

"The 'lady's fingernail' is like my lady's fingernail.
I admire the 'lady's curtain' but yearn instead for my lady's curtain.
I see the *chomphu* and is it not my young one's shawl,[128] delicately
    hanging?
The rings of these beautiful trees cannot compare with the circlets
    of my great one's neck. (257)

Phra Lo continued upon his journey, admiring the great variety of
trees along both sides of his route. The *yang* alighted in the *yang*,
admiring their flocks. The *yung* landed in the *yung*, teasing one
another. The *plao* perched in the *plao*, in wondrous flocks. The *kasa*
sought out the *kasang*. The *rang* was festooned with the nests of the
rangnan. The peahen climbed about the cockscomb. The bamboo
alighted in pairs in the bamboo. The *totto* alighted in the *tot*. The
tapkha jumped about in the *kha*. The *khla* alighted in the *khla*, as the
wa did in the *wa*, and the *khapkhae* in the *khaepa*. The lotus pecked
among the lotus. The parrots and cockatoos climbed back and forth
in the many trees. In boundless groups and countless flocks, they took
to the air in flight, calling out to one another. (258)[129]

The *ka* alighted in the vines of the *tumka* tree.
The *ka* passed through the *kala* tree. The *ka* soared, calling out.
Flocks of *ka* came to alight on the *pheka* tree.
The *ka* turned away from the *matka* tree, brushing the twigs and
    branches of the *kalong* tree. (259)[130]

The tiger crept past the "tiger's eye" tree, eyeing the roadway.

The deer stole up to the "deer's ear" trees, concealing themselves.

The elephants bent the thickets of bamboo and *sang* grass, hiding
themselves.[131]

The elephants passed playfully through the "elephant cane,"
disappearing into the deep woods. (260)[132]

Monkeys swung through the "monkey's ladder"
and watched the young monkeys climb down to pluck fruit.

The "breeze monkey" chased the breezes, leaping about playfully.

Young monkeys chased and jumped and cavorted in the "monkey's
ladder." (261)[133]

The *huat, hiang, hat, haen, han.* The *chanchuang, chancheng, chik.* The
pring, prong, prik, pru, prang. The *khui, khe, khang, kho, khet.* The
stands of *phlet* trees and *phlong* trees. The groves of *fong* trees and
fai trees. The clusters of *phai* trees and *pho* trees. The *tako* trees and
the *taku.* The *lamphu* trees and the *lampheng.* The stands of *daeng*
trees and the *dan.* The *somphan* trees and the *saraphi.* The *nonsi* and
the *tharabun.* The *khun, kamkun,* and *kamyan.* The *phiman* trees, the
khlaw, and the *khlai.* The *kamchai* and *chambok.* The *kathokrok,* the
sak, and the *son.* And all these trees are only those that come to mind.
There were also many others. (262)[134]

Vines and creepers climbed the trees.

Suspended, entwined and blended in with the leaves, tips curled,
leaves beautiful. (263)

Profuse blossoms hung down in bunches

With a fragrance that bathed and infused all, intensifying sadness
  for his loved one. (264)

"Thinking of what is behind and fearing for what lies ahead,
My heart is driven to distraction because I have abandoned my love
  to come here." (265)

The king continued his travels for many days and many nights until
he reached the boundary of the royal territory. There, among the
trees, they established a royal encampment, beautiful and admirable
in every way. The department officers and ministers attended the
king, in all their great numbers. The royal King Lo then spoke forth,
thus: (266)

["I am going to go for a long time.
Oh, all of you return to your happy homes."] (267)[135]

"I have traveled for a long time to reach the limits of my realm.
It is proper that I send my great force back to their homes.
I have compassion for all, separated from their wives and children.
For my part, I think about the noble Phuean and golden
  Phaeng." (268)

All the ministers saluted the king.
"Upon our heads we place the dust from beneath your royal foot.[136]
We ask that you linger and set your heart at ease.
Wait three or four days, oh royal lord, and then let your forces
  return." (269)

[Phra Lo replied,] "It has been too long for comfort, my ministers.

Setting out tomorrow will be most fitting, so make no delay.

If it is too long our capital will be bereft.

The revered lady awaits word of us. (270)

They raised their hands in salute at the feet of the king,

their raised hands standing like flowers.

"You have been like a father to us, dear sovereign.

You have formed all that is noble in us. (271)

"We ask to follow you, our dharma king,

until you once again return to ascend your throne.

If we should go and meet our fates, it would still be better than
   returning.

In whatever difficulty you face, make use of us, your servants who
   wish to assist you." (272)

[Phra Lo replied,] "As I go ahead, I feel that I want to go back.

I fear for my kingdom, and I fear for my queen.

You who know how I govern my realm,

govern every area and leave no one in want. (273)

"I entrust to you my city, my elephants and horses, my subjects, and
   my royal army.

I entrust to you all in my domain, both the inner and outer reaches.

Do not neglect your responsibilities. Diligently assess right and
   wrong.

I entrust to you the revered queen of the land, and I entrust my
   precious companion in love." (274)

He instructed his ministers in detail, in every department.

They received his exalted words,
tears flowing forth for love of him.
"We beg of you, great king, be not long in returning." (275)

[Phra Lo replied,] "When you reach her majesty, the queen mother,
advise her that I, her child,
have found happiness and live in peace
and that I incline my head in salute to her. (276)

"And then go and salute the great queen.
Say, 'I have found happiness and am not ill.
I shall hasten to rejoin you, my precious wife.
Do not weep and sob. Be ready to receive me on my return.'" (277)

He had them select and prepare a group of one hundred of those who were close and familiar to him to follow him in his travels. The rest, ministers and subjects alike, along with elephants and horses, he bade make their return. "But with you two, my attendants, I shall go on. Seek out those who know the ways of the people of this outpost and who can spread knowledge of our good will and regard.[137] Once you are close to them in friendship, then reveal our intentions. Give them gold, silver, and articles of clothing to win their confidence. Then speak to them pleasingly, and when they are on our side say that the king deigns to present royal rewards, gold and silver enough to satisfy the heart. Tell them not to conceal things but to inform us fully. I will pose as the outpost chief, and you, my attendants, as assistants of the rank of *muen*. The swordsmen will take on the rank of *phan*. The rest of you will be as commoners. Change your name, each of you. Address each other as the local people do. Be attentive, watching carefully as you pass along the roadways. Discover all that is hidden. Keep your real intent from spreading out, and so make your disguise convincing. Greet all those you encounter. When you approach a forest village if they question you, respond artfully and tell them of my fame, saying that I have come from the royal city to travel the far reaches of the territory and that I will then return. Regale them thus in detail. Omit nothing, so that all is exact and clear in accordance with this ruse." (278)

[They responded to Phra Lo,] "May your merit be upon us, royal one. The strategy you have devised is pleasingly correct in every way." (279)

And the royal one set off immediately.
Taking just his two attendants, the king departed. (280)

Having reached the entrance to the forest,
they spoke as though inviting each other to venture deep within
   it. (281)

"We salute and take our leave of your royal highness."
Taking only the two attendants with him the king went in. (282)

Then he passed through the populated areas with his attendants leading the way. He set aside his identity as a meritorious lord and conducted himself as the chieftain of a remote area. He wore a hat and fine clothing, hiding himself from view. (283)

He passed along through the vast forest
and there were horsemen, and mahouts, and the monarch and his
   attendants, in three groups. (284)

Following behind his two attendants the king made his way, dwelling for a time in each hamlet. Emerging from the forest, they came upon a group of important local officials. Following their plan, they engaged these local people in conversation. Seeing Phra Lo arrive among them they inquired about him and were told his name and pedigree, that he was a chieftain from the capital traveling the far reaches of the territory, then to return. Bringing items to present to him, the local people visited with the lord. From the hamlet at the entry to the forest to each of the hamlets the exalted one went without delay. (285)

Coming to the Kalong River he dismounted his elephant close to the bank, and there they sat to rest. He had wood cut to tie together to form a raft. Then, when he had crossed the river he had a place cleared for an encampment, one fit for a local chieftain. The exalted royal one bathed and washed his hair. When he had cleansed his royal hair the king's thoughts returned to his exalted mother. (286)

[Phra Lo said,] "Oh, how sad.
Perhaps, my queen, you are weeping for me now. (287)

"The pain of love and the pain of separation are difficult pains to
    treat,
and so it is with the pain of longing to return home.
You are suffering because I have ventured here alone.
And the pain in your heart, dear lady, brings pain to me. (288)

"You have suffered pain for my father, and now also for me.
You suffer alone in pitiable pain.
You suffer pain for fear of disgrace from our royal enemies.
These pains intensify ceaselessly and make me wish for death. (289)

"Can a hundred lovers compare with the flesh of one's own wife?
Can a thousand wives equal one's mother?
Can it be easy to carry a child, and to give it birth?
To raise a child is difficult, oh my queen. (290)

"Should I not go on but turn back and go home
to see Her Majesty Bunluea?
My misery is overwhelming. I beg that you help me to consider—
what misdeed has left me in such distress?" (291)

And the two attendants raised their hands in salute to him and respectfully hastened to speak saying, "You have told us that you will return to your great city. We support your wish. You need not go in secret. You should return to govern your domain together with her highness the younger lady, and the excellent noble, your mother." (292)

[Phra Lo replied,] "If I go on I shall become a stranger among
scoundrels.
If I go back people may speak ill of me,
saying that their lord is a coward,
adding disgrace to my suffering. Oh, I would be better off dead." (293)

The two attendants hastened to respond,
saying, "Who could dare to criticize you, even to the extent of a
strand of hair?" (294)

[Phra Lo replied,] "I shall go for just a short time and then return.
What is before me remains, and what is behind me remains. I am
drawn to both.
I fear only that their spirits may compel me to stay,

Preventing me from returning to see my lady, the queen. (295)

"Come, I shall seek an omen in these rushing waters.
This river named Kalong flows in great volume.
If I am to go on yet not escape to return in safety,
may the waters whirl in a circle. If I am to be safe, may they flow
     freely on." (296)

As soon as his words had passed his lips, the waters circled
and then turned red, as though stained with blood.
His heart was beset with a terrible suffering
as though crushed beneath a tree trunk a hundred spans in girth. (297)

He did not let the others know but concealed all.
Rising from his bath, he went to his bed.
He entered the victory pavilion thinking, "How can it have come to
     this?"
Closing the curtain, he sobbed, "Oh Bunluea, my revered lady." (298)

[He thought to himself] "Should you die, may I yet see to your
     remains.
Should I die, my mother and queen, may you see to mine.
Cremate my remains and leave me not in disgrace.
Or shall it be that I cannot cremate your remains nor you cremate
     mine? (299)

"If I am to die, then I will die.
But I am pained that I will not again see my mother's face." (300)

Tears flooded down with his sobs,

becoming blood falling to his burning breast. "Oh mother, you shall
not see me again! (301)

"I have seen a terrible omen in the water.
Oh, my lady, my breast is aching, and I am brought low. (302)

"I am a ruler with rank surpassing the skies.
By what misdeed am I brought low that I face my end alone? (303)

"I could not turn back, even if I wanted to.
I have ventured too far from my home, oh royal one. (304)

"I have been an earthly ruler and a heavenly lord.
The kings of one hundred and one royal cities have attended me.

But now I am alone in the middle of this great river.
I may never see your face again, my lady, nor you mine." (305)

His suffering was as vast as the skies. He pondered what lay before
him and what lay behind. He composed himself, concealing his
suffering with a cheerful manner. Pretending to be light at heart he
opened the curtains and called the people of the outpost to consult
with him. "Take my two attendants, as close to me as my own life, to
seek out places where I should stay. That which should be hidden
from view, do so, to give all a pleasing appearance. Whatever must be
done in secret, do it so, and with clever artifice. Map out the routes
and the turns along the way. Remember the names of the hamlets,
places for assembling troops, elephants and horses. Look both ahead
and behind, both near and far. Examine all with eye and heart. And
you, my attendants, consider carefully every detail of our plan." (306)

Having received this order from the monarch,
they saluted at his feet and then set out. (307)

They did not deviate from their lord's orders
but inspected all the places and all the routes, memorizing every
    detail. (308)

They led the two attendants into all the secret places
and they [Kaew and Khwan] befriended those living in all the
    villages along the way. (309)

They offered inducements for assistance, and
even those unyielding as iron were drawn out by silver and
    softened. (310)

Having won their confidence,
Khwan and Kaew began their ploy, speaking with sweet-sounding
    words. (311)

They explained all to them in detail,
and the local people said, "Don't be concerned. Leave these matters
    to us." (312)

The two of them went in to see the pleasure garden, giving bribes to
the caretakers to win them over. Gold and silver sealed their lips and
made them useful in many ways. The two of them went to see the
gates of the palace and saw even the residence of the two princesses.
That which might stand in the way, they saw clearly. That which might
be of assistance, they saw fully. They examined everything, taking

care with each detail. Never letting on to anyone, they kept their deception hidden, concealing their ruse. (313)

Passing carefully along the route and lingering in each village, the two men grew familiar with the forest path. With heads held high they made their way and eventually approached their destination. Then pressing quickly on they reached their king. They saluted him and told him the results of their artifice, of all the hidden and secret things they had seen. They drew out maps to show him everything in detail. (314)

The king considered all carefully and then spoke. "Leave two elephants and four horses here with the outpost officers." He selected exactly thirty courageous and able men to accompany him. The remaining seventy stayed behind with the elephants and horses. The king then waited in anticipation of an auspicious time and day. The two attendants listened to the royal orders in full, ready to respond. (315)

At that same time, the two princesses
waited, looking for some sign of the exalted one.
"Oh, Ruen and Roy, the king isn't coming!
If you love us go quickly and remind our venerable lord. (316)

And so, they went to remind the lord of the great mountains.
He told them, "Phra Lo has come to the river's edge.
On the banks of the Kalong he is impatiently awaiting the proper
    day.
Come, I will again entice him to hurry." (317)

He concentrated upon the wild forest cocks, calling them in his mind, and they came in countless clusters and flocks. He selected one of beauty—young, supple, and strong. Its hackles were a brilliant red and its feathers a lustrous shimmering green. Its wings were a progression of the five colors[138] glistening like the foot of the precious swan.[139] The rims of its eyes were a beautiful vermillion and its handsome comb shone in the light. It crowed with a sound that captured the heart. Its curved spurs were brilliant orange. Its feet were like the purest gold, etched with vermillion and painted with yellow. He ordered a spirit to take possession of the precious cock, and so it showed no fear. It raised its head boldly and danced excitedly about, beating its wings and crowing loudly with a sound that gladdened the ear. The venerable one instructed the cock in detail, and in a moment it sprung up and leapt away. Swiftly it drew near the radiant King Lo and raised its head to crow, beating its wings as it strutted about. It called softly, pleasingly, and spread forth its wings and tail, comely and beautiful. The sight of this entrancing figure, attractive in every way, opened the king's heart. Without pausing to apply his perfumes, put on his crown and raiment, or take up the royal victory weapons, he rushed out in pursuit, intending to capture the beautiful cock. The others broke camp and followed the great king. Whenever he lost the trail, the cock stopped to wait. Whenever he was slow in tracking it, the cock crowed to call him. But the cock kept a wary eye on him, and whenever he came close, the cock went further on, going at a moderate pace, moving rhythmically, walking gracefully as a swan. Whenever it saw that they were separated, though, the cock stopped. And when they then approached the limits of the forest and were about to pass into a settlement, the cock feigned exhaustion. Seeing the cock moving slowly he stepped toward it, but it took flight and disappeared from sight. The king looked gloomily in all directions and thought to himself, "Oh, I have been deceived by this cock. It is possessed by a spirit, and it has tricked me." He turned to look to his attendants, who spoke with soothing words. (318)

[Kaew and Khwan said,] "From now on you must be cautious and not forget yourself. You must inform everyone before you set out." When he neared the home of some who were favorably inclined, they passed the word along quietly, calling the country people to come to greet him and invite the king to enter those places that were suitable. Then they presented him with sustenance and invited him to seek his pleasure there for the night. And there he left behind ten men. When he reached the next hamlet, he left five men and elephants. And so those who accompanied him numbered only fifteen. Further on ahead he left behind ten more. Reaching another hamlet there were empty gardens with no one present, and a vast forest of pines fading into the distance. There was an empty and solitary dwelling too, and they invited the monarch to abide there, not far from the garden of the princesses. They raised hands respectfully in salutation and arrayed themselves about him in attendance. (319)

Greeting him with respectful words, they presented food, perfumed water for bathing, and water to drink. They gave him a clean mattress, sheets, and pillows, and a spread of silk, inquiring of his attendants about each point, so the furnishings would all be in order. And the king comported himself as a Brahmin bearing the name Lord Sri Ket, who had come from the land of the self-created one[140] and was desirous of seeing the country. And his attendants, in the guise of laymen bearing the names Rat and Ram, reminded all of them not to speak carelessly about these secret matters. And out of affection for them, the local people invited the two attendants and the soldiers to go to their dwelling places. There they presented food and liquor to them. They said, "Please, companions of the lord, our brothers, partake of this." (320)

They provided for all of them everywhere in the hamlet. At the approach of evening the king desired to see the princesses' garden. They pointed out the way, and the king set forth without delay. (321)

> The watchmen in attendance
> spread news of the king's arrival in the pleasure garden. (322)

> They encouraged each other to approach and greet him
> and to invite him to take his leisure in the royal garden. (323)

> The king's face beamed.
> He admired the flowers and the trees and the fruit, all pleasing to his
> heart. (324)

> He viewed the surroundings
> and said, "Oh, I thank you for your generosity." (325)

> "Whose garden could this be? I would like to know."
> [The locals responded,] "It is the garden of the lovely princesses. (326)

> And they then composed a verse
> in honor of the meritorious king. (327)

> "As your servants, we salute at your feet, admirable one.
> Please, excellent sir, admire the garlands of flowers
> in this pleasure garden of tranquil charm.

All is happiness in the princesses' garden of leisure." (328)

The king admired the incomparable fragrance of the *karaket*
    blossom,
its scent like the stimulating bouquet of scented hair.[141]
He admired the jasmine, stirred by its enchanting bouquet.
He admired the flowers, grown for the hair braids of noble Phuean
    and golden Phaeng. (329)

The "lady's smile" was as his lady's smile, enticing to him.
The waving leaves were beckoning arms, gesturing to him.
The "lady's hairpiece" wafting in the breeze; was it not waving to him?
They invited the king to admire the many trees, their branches
    bending in salutation. (330)

The many birds perched upon the many trees, arrayed throughout,
calling out continuously, welcoming the exalted lord.
The *krasa* bird called out in joy at seeing Phra Lo
and alighted on the *kasang* tree, playfully tugging at its mate. (331)

The parrot played in the parrot tree seeking love,
calling to the great and exalted king.
The *sattawa* sent out its call, inviting him, and
the *khla* bird paired with its mate, expressing its love. (332)[142]

They invited the king to admire the ponds,
to admire the blossoming lotus, slowly blooming.
Crabs and fish and turtles moved about in great abundance.
The carpenter bee caressed the flowers, penetrating the
    blossoms. (333)

The king made his way and seated himself.
He thought about the young princesses, the noble Phuean and
    golden Phaeng. (334)

His attendants invited him to take his rest:
"Darkness has come, and evening breezes caress the trees."
Keening in lament, the lord spoke out in verses of grief. (335)

"You princesses are as life is to me.
I left my glorious city and hastened here.
Not seeing you disappoints me.
Oh, I think about you and I yearn for you. (336)

"Smitten, I yearn for you, who are like fragrant flowers.
The fragrance of the *lamduan* is so like the scent of my beloved
    ones.
The god of the winds blows, stirring my heart to greater pining.
The moon fills the clear sky with its light, and still I am not united
    with you. (337)

"The perfume of the *maluli* and the *maliwan*,
the aroma of the *pru* and *prayong* inflame my five desires.[143]
This bouquet is like your scent.
Oh, I smell your perfume but cannot see your faces. I would that I
    were dead. (338)

"The redolence of the flowers leaves me empty hearted.
I see the many birds throughout the forests.
Oh birds, take a message to present to them.
Let the young sisters have word of me. (339)

"Myna, I beg you, carry a message for me.

Inform the sisters

that I have passed through great difficulty to find them.

I hear the birds calling, as I am crying out in passionate longing. (340)

"*Sattawa*, I beg you to hasten to them.

Bring them news of me, far from their precious fragrance

and lingering here in this royal garden,

so that they will know the place where I await them. (341)

"Oh *noori*, hurry, take wing and make your way.

Go to the golden dwelling of the delicate nobles.

Relate my message of invitation to the two dear princesses

to come and enjoy the trees in this peaceful arbor. (342)

"Oh barbet and cuckoo, you call out pleasingly.

Your harmonies beguile my heart.

Beloved birds, hasten to the lovely princesses.

Bid them come to this festive garden to satisfy my urgent

longing. (343)

"The birds soar about in the air, crying out.

Alighting in the trees they conceal themselves and hide.

But they bring me no news of the princesses.

Some move about in the trees, some dance about, crowded together

calling out." (344)

Phra Lo observed the birds, listening indifferently, while his attendants massaged his feet. With gestures of reverent respect, they said, "Be not afflicted so. Tomorrow you will join with the charming princesses." (345)

They invited him to recline upon the jeweled dais.
The cicadas' unbroken call lulled the lord, lightening his mood. (346)

The breezes bore the fragrance of the flowers,
and the lord was immersed in the scent of the noble ones. (347)

A radiant moon shone down upon the earth,
and the king longed to look upon the faces of the princesses. (348)

In his heart Phra Lo was pleased and at rest, refreshed by the words
    of his attendants,
who, speaking to him in smoothly polished verse, lulled their lord to
    sleep. (349)

The two of them then lay down in sleep at his feet, and the king dreamed.
Khwan and Kaew also slept and dreamed their own separate dreams.
The king then suddenly awoke, and rousing his attendants quickly
related his dream, bidding them help to interpret its meaning. (350)

"Listen, Kaew! Hear me, Khwan!
You lulled me to sleep and then I dreamed.
In my dream I wore breast chains, colored as the complexion of the
    princesses.
My breasts were encircled, but just this moment I awoke in
    distress. (351)

"In my dream, I embraced my loved ones.
I dreamed that they had come to my jeweled dais.
In my sleep, I rose and searched for them.

I dreamed that I was caught in a snare, tightly bound in my
    desire. (352)

"I dreamed that I wore clothing of the freshest and purest cloth.
In my hair were fragrant flowers.
I went in the direction of the sunrise, and
I dreamt the delicate ones played about in the great pond. (353)

"I dreamed that with my right hand I fondled a precious lotus
while embracing another with my left.
The carp roiled the water in pursuit of the murrell.[144]
Jumping joyfully, the golden *phruan* fish glided among the flowers
    in the great pond." (354)

The two attendants then interpreted the king's dream. "It will come
to pass as you have imagined it, oh lord. Do not be saddened, for
tomorrow you will unite with them, daughters of a meritorious
lord." (355)

Kaew then told of his own dream.
"I dreamed that you, my king, rose to admire the moon in the
    cloudless skies.
Two moons spread colorful light, each one beautiful.
Oh king, you will unite with the young princesses, as beautiful as the
    lotus." (356)

Khwan had dreamed that the king was like the moon,
carried aloft by young goddesses.
"I dreamed that you were pleased and had satisfied your heart's
    desires.

> Oh king, you will soon unite with these young ladies of royal
>   blood." (357)

As his attendants related these portents of good fortune, the king's
mood eased. He spoke in appreciation of their dreams and felt as
though the princesses had come themselves to calm him, satisfying
his desires. (358)

[But] pity the princesses, Phuean and Phaeng, perfect as the blossoms
of a flower, who retired to their jeweled sleeping chamber worried
and bereft, and wrapped their arms about themselves and sobbed
because their love was long in coming. (359)

Fearing that they would not attain their desires, their cheeks trembled
and their hair swayed back and forth. The two were bewildered and
sad, watching continuously for the king. Weeping through endless
hours, they bathed themselves in currents of tears. Quietly they
whispered to their ladies-in-waiting, "That which we desire has
eluded us. If we cannot unite with our loved one, tomorrow we shall
die!" (360)

With respectful gestures to the two princesses, the ladies-in-waiting
consoled them. They comforted the two royal daughters, saying, "We
have not yet passed the allotted time. Please, restrain yourselves and
wait. Before long, your beloved lord will come unite with you. (361)

> "Do not be troubled by your yearning. If not today, then tomorrow
>   morning
> King Lo will make his way into the lovely pleasure garden." (362)

[Phra Phuean and Phra Phaeng replied,] "Just how do you know, older ones? What person has come to report to you this news of the exalted lord? Has the king really come?" (363)

The ladies-in-waiting gestured respectfully and replied, "Dear highnesses, the aged one, imbued with power, has given us knowledge of the omens to be found in flocks of birds, showing us which of them portend good and which misfortune. The signs are that great happiness will soon come, without delay. We, your servants, are as pleased as if the handsome king had already made his way to your sides, where we could see him with our own eyes." (364)

The two princesses were greatly pleased and thanked their ladies-in-waiting for their words. "We hold your message in a position of honor. You are of great value to us. We will wait, but we intend to repay your kindness. (365)

"From the time we were small, you, our ladies-in-waiting,
have been of value beyond expression.
And in this matter also it is fitting that you help us.
If you can help us unite with the king your value will be
    unsurpassed." (366)

After hearing these heartening words of praise,
the ladies-in-waiting spoke soothing words to the princesses. (367)

"Be not concerned, precious ones. Please take your rest with an easy
    heart. Before long, princesses, King Lo will appear. (368)

"Be not troubled. Sleep and await Phra Lo, and we will comfort you with music." Hearing these words, the princesses reclined. The ladies-in-waiting embraced their feet and sang to comfort them. "Sleep soundly, sleep, oh princesses. (369)

"This radiant golden dais shines with the luster of jewels.
Mattress of embroidered silk, pillows with sparkling gems.
Elegant cushions and headrests, and a canopy decorated with
    abundant stars.
Curtains and drapes carefully made to protect you. (370)

"Sleep, you royal sisters.
Delicate souls, be neither concerned nor upset.
Phra Lo will come to unite with you.
Do not be aggrieved, and wait in patience. (371)

"Oh flowing breezes, invite the king to come here.
Blow through the skies to reach him.
May the heavenly gods hasten him.
May the moon and all the stars be as torches illuminating his
    journey." (372)

They listened as the ladies-in-waiting sang.
They sang that the radiant Phra Lo would come.
Sweet to the ear and pleasing to the heart,
the melodious sound lulled them to sleep. (373)

The princesses having fallen to sleep,
their ladies-in-waiting, singing to soothe their ladies, themselves fell
    asleep. (374)

And in due course the four of them dreamed and saw miraculous omens, which stayed pleasingly in their thoughts. Immediately upon awakening Phra Phuean related her dream and interpreted its hidden meaning. (375)

"I dreamed that celestial blossoms came to my hands,
in fragrance and beauty without equal,
auspicious garlands, the finest in the world,
heavenly ornaments, to be placed atop our heads." (376)

Pleased beyond expression,
Phaeng, close by her side, related her own dream. (377)

"I dreamed that the sun god came
to become a pin for my hair, placed at the center of my head.
The moon became my mirror.
The many stars were arrayed about my head like flowers in my
   hair." (378)

The ladies-in-waiting praised these dreams. "You ladies will achieve what your hearts intend and attain your desires. You will bathe in the thousand streams[145] and be royal queens of Phra Lo, illustrious with rank and dignity and fortunate before the world. The handsome King Lo will come to embrace you ladies, uniting with you in love." (379)

[Phuean and Phaeng said,] "May it come to pass according to your
   blessings.
Listening to you two is as if you had given us a heaven of our
   own." (380)

Roy was gladdened and pleased. Ruen raised her hands in respect, saluting at the feet of the young princesses. The two ladies-in-waiting, gesturing respectfully, spoke. (381)

> Ruen related her own dream:
> "I dreamed that you had arranged the stars about your heads.
> I dreamed that a serpent had encircled its loved one, nearly
>   devouring it.
> King Lo will come here quickly to visit both of you." (382)

> Roy said to them, "I also joined with you in dreaming.
> I dreamed that you attained a heavenly kingdom.
> You both partook of divine elixir, sharing the essence together.
> Lo, the exalted king shall arrive tomorrow." (383)

> When they had finished interpreting these encouraging dreams,
> night was dispersing before the early morning light.
> As the dawn came to the sky, the princesses waited.
> To them, the coming of the day seemed to take a thousand
>   years. (384)

They heard the calls of birds, the *duwao*, the *khao*, the *katha*, and the *phuradok*. The *khokma* turned to each other. The *sunok* called lustily, and the *kaikaew* called continuously as though saying, "At dawn's first light you may go to visit the king within the pleasure garden." (385)

The moon had shed its light, and the sun rose into the sky. The woodpecker and the thrush circled about and alighted among the great trees, calling forth the news that the noble one had come. Hearing the crow calling out the news of the lord's arrival, the ladies-in-waiting praised the good omens and told the princesses that the birds calls were a sign. "Wondrous things are at hand, oh our royal highnesses. You are soon to meet the great king!" (386)

The princesses were refreshed and gladdened.
"Oh Roy and Ruen, don't delay. Hurry on your way!" (387)

They two turned skillfully to their task. They prepared themselves, and taking their leave they mounted an elephant and set out. As for Phra Lo, when it was morning, he gave directions to the keepers of the royal garden, "If any should come to ask you who came here, you must say, 'Foreign men, two in number, and a Brahmin, for a total of three, came together and asked to sleep here until the dawn. Looking upon the flower garden they sighed a great sigh. And when morning came, they took their leave, departing just a short while ago.'" When he had finished his instructions, the king set off. (388)

The king's attendants looked carefully about. Turning back, they saw two women making their way along the road. The women dismounted their elephants and went into the royal garden. Quickly they asked the garden caretakers, "Has anyone come here?" The attendants replied as the lord had instructed, and the women deliberated and said, "You saw them. So, you tell us. Were they young or old? And what did they look like?" The caretakers replied, "They are without compare! Even a divinity could not be the equal of these most handsome and beautiful youths. Merely seeing the Brahmin engenders love and desire. And of the two who were following him, oh, have no interest in them, for they have no equal." The two listened and were sorely vexed. "Oh, how infuriating! We spent too much time in preparation. If we had hurried instead, we would not have been left here in doubt." (389)

The two were heartsick.
"Ah! What a pity! We have come just a bit too late. (390)

"And how can we arrange
to see them? Help us and we will reward you! (391)

"Now is our opportunity. Quickly!
It can't be anyone other than the king and his attendants." (392)

They peered until their eyes were dry,
and in the distance they saw two handsome ones. They went
    cautiously, following each other. (393)

[Ruen and Roy said to the caretakers,] "Come quickly and look. This
is who you told us about a moment ago, is it not?" (394)

The caretakers looked and then replied, "Yes, certainly.
The two men coming yonder are the friends of the virtuous
    Brahmin." (395)

The two women quickly crept up near them,
and they contrived to pass by unnoticed, avoiding being seen. (396)

[Ruen and Roy said to each other,] "Oh, this has been truly easy.
We have succeeded. How wonderful!" (397)

The two went down secretly into the pond
to steal a glimpse of them from hiding. "Don't let them see us." (398)

The two men arrived without delay,

and as they neared they slowed to an ostentatious walk. (399)

Walking with extended arms they put on airs,
entering from the front of the pleasure garden. (400)

[Kaew and Khwan said,] "Those people we saw walking by just a
    moment ago,
where have they disappeared to without letting us see them? (401)

"This certainly is strange.
We have looked and looked, but there is no one anywhere." (402)

The two men then went down into the pond, and there they encoun-
tered the two women, who with broad smiles laughed gently. They
waited and when the two men came close, they feigned ignorance
and questioned them. (403)

"What territory do you two men come from?
You who are arrogant enough to come with no thought or
    consideration.
You dare even to come into the royal pond?
Get out of here! If you don't leave, you will regret it!" (404)

[Kaew and Khwan replied,] "We will go, but ladies, don't drive us
    away.
We have traveled here from a distant city.
Seeing this pleasant pond, we desired to admire it.
We meant no harm. Ladies, don't be so hasty in threatening us. (405)

"We came into this garden

and saw not a single person tending it.

We saw this inviting pond and wished to bathe ourselves.

We did not know that there were ladies here to criticize and shame
us. (406)

"We take our leave of you, dear and lovely ones.

If we were to stay our shame would be even greater than it is now.

To be men driven away by women is a disgrace.

It was only because we did not see you that we came down here." (407)

[Ruen and Roy replied,] "Oh sirs, be not so quick to anger.

We made a small mistake, and you return it a thousand-fold with
contemptuous words.

It might have been disreputable men who wandered in here—that is
why we spoke as we did.

We were wrong because we did not see, so please forgive us." (408)

[Kaew and Khwan replied,] "If we had seen you [and still entered
the pond] you should be angry.

But we didn't see you, so should your anger equal even a strand of a
hair?

Listening to you is a strong elixir that freshens our hearts.

If our words have offended you ladies, please do not be angry." (409)

[Ruen and Roy replied] "If you wish to bathe please come into the
water.

Come bathe in the pond and cool yourselves.

Scrub away the dust and dirt and wash away the sweat and grime.

Then pick the lotus, peel away its covering and eat of the fruit." (410)

The two men listened to the two women. They changed their clothing while going down to bathe. Conducting themselves politely and with good manners, they spoke with careful words, chosen to please. "Bathing in this pond is like bathing in precious celestial water, oh exalted ones. (411)

"The lotus flowers are truly delicious,
a heavenly delicacy, because of your hospitality. (411a)[146]

"The red[147] lotus is delicious. Oh, it captures the heart.
And the white lotus, how is it? We wish to know."
[Ruen and Roy said,] "Feel free to go among the lotus clusters.
You will find a taste like a divine nectar. You needn't seek for it in the
    heavens." (412)

[Ruen said to Roy,] "Mistress Roy, if you feel love, do not be
    hesitant.
Lead our guest among the lotus.
Whatever he wishes to gather or eat, follow his inclination.
Help him in his gathering, mistress, and do so with a willing
    heart." (413)

Lady Roy called with beautiful words.
She was enticing, like the god of love.
They followed each other passing into the lotus leaves, lush and
    thick.
The scent of the lotus, and the fragrance of her cheeks—her cheeks
    surpassed the lotus. (414)

[Khwan said,] "I am grateful to the concealing lotus leaves.

The blossoms seem to laugh, summoning me.
Enraptured, I caress the lotus, with deep admiration,
Just as I admire my lady, together with me. (415)

"Lotus breasts, lotus eyes, smiling lotus face.
Spreading lotus fragrance, aromatic, sweet, stimulating essence.
Lotus breasts stir my heart to breaking.
Beautiful lotus feet. From feet to precious hair, truly beautiful." (416)

"Oh, red lotus, filled with love, my precious great lotus.
The fragrant lotus scent mimics the scent of my precious one.
My desirous one, join me in mingling the scents.
Let us gather without ceasing, joining together in our sport." (417)

"Oh joy! Oh my lotus, concealed amid the lotus blossoms."
The murrel prodded the majestic flower.
The *salit*, *pho*, and *taphian* fish came together in rapturous
admiration.
They crowded together to prod the bank, seeking prey, and in the
frenzy were bathed in foam. (418)

Pleasure on this side, pressing close to his heart's desire,
And pleasure also on that side, for the other two.
What pleasure could be like this?
They cavorted back and forth in their hidden places, exciting their
partner's desires. (419)

Having found pleasure in the water, they sought pleasure on the
land.
The two pairs joined happily in climbing out of the pond.

They came up, embracing and kissing,
and their pleasure returned, filling the earth and sky with the
    intensity of their passion. (420)

The two women led their guests to the garden dwelling.
They brushed the mattress and spread sheets and invited them to
    continue their enjoyment.
The two pairs coupled; they laughed, and they joined together again.
And together they knew the heights of desire. (421)

After their coupling, their passion fulfilled,
the two gently asked the names of their lovers.
"Where do you two come from and how are you known? Tell us,
    dear ones,
so that we may know your names and that of your city." (422)

The two listened to the women but, speaking with deception, did not
reveal their names. "Our names are Ram and Rat. We came together
to engage in trade. In our wanderings, we came to a junction in the
roadway, and there we met a Brahmin lord, by name Sri Ket, and
wishing to see this country, we came along. And then we met you,
beautiful ones, our great loves. (423)

"We live in a city abounding in pleasure, a charming royal capitol,
home to many delights. But we declare that we will stay with you.
From now on, we will not leave." (424)

The two women were astonished.
This went beyond their expectations. How should they respond? (425)

[Ruen and Roy replied,] "You came to this city,
but what did you bring to trade? We would like to know!" (426)

The handsome men were far apart and had no time to consult with
    each other.
The women questioned them relentlessly and they were abashed. (427)

"Quickly! Tell us about your wares!
Hah! You have no answer! Ridiculous! (428)

"You have concealed your identity,
yet you don't appear untrustworthy or trying to take advantage
    of us. (429)

"You'd have goods enough to sell, would you not? Or would say the
cost was beyond you? You have not been truthful and are hiding
something, aren't you? By your bearing you are noblemen, are you
not? You are not lowborn, but are palace born, no? Your mien is not
that of merchants, not that of common men. (430)

"Come, let us laugh to forget our hunger.
Please, gentlemen, speak the truth to us. Don't hide anything." (431)

They replied to the women's questioning.
"Don't ridicule us. We will tell you the truth. (432)

"His highness
King Lo has made his way here. We, his attendants, have
    accompanied him." (433)

When the men had related this news,

the women thrilled, as if a kingdom had come into their
    possession. (434)

[Ruen and Roy replied,] "The sun, descended from the heavens, has
    come to rest in our hands.

If we wished to take hold of the moon, we could now do so.

If we should wish to leap the golden Meru, we could safely do so.

Please, invite the royal one, lord and king, to come. (435)

"In what place does the king reside?

In whose garden is he staying? We must know!"

[Kaew and Khwan replied,] "He has gone into an empty garden.

Alone and without companions, he has come alone." (436)

Ruen and Roy struck their breasts and called out, "Oh royal king,

how can you live so pitiably?

Never could you have experienced such difficulty. How lonely you
    must be!"

They cried and sobbed, awash with tears. (437)

"Oh, have pity! Both of you, hurry to him.

When you reach him, attend him and salute in respect at his feet.

Respectfully invite the great king to make his way here,

and we will invite the two noble princesses to come in all haste. (438)

"But first we must stay in wait for the king,

bowing with hands raised high in salutation.

We wish to receive his words to take

to the princesses, who are awaiting news." (439)

The two men took the two women into their arms,
their hands embracing their slender waists, caressing their midriffs.
They looked in admiration while kissing them. "We tell you, dear
    ones,
we do not want to be separated from you, even for a moment." (440)

The two women pressed tightly to the flesh of the two men.
"Noble ones, you are about to leave us.
Parting is a death.
If you love us, hurry back. Spare us, and do not be long." (441)

They had gone only two or three paces when they turned back,
[Kaew and Khwan said,] "Oh beloved ones, already we are separated
    from you.
We go only in body to find the great king.
Our hearts stay here to admire you." (442)

[Ruen and Roy said,] "We feel as you do.
We remain here only in body. In our hearts, we follow you.
Go, and be not long in returning to us.
Please hasten your return. If you linger, we shall perish." (443)

The men went without delay.
Reaching their majestic king, they prostrated and informed him of
    the news. (444)

[They informed him of every point,
describing from the beginning every detail of the events.] (445)[148]

"We have met the princesses' ladies-in-waiting.

They await you, beloved king.
They beg to invite you, oh pinnacle, Siva king, saying
'Exalted royal lord, please do not delay setting forth.'" (446)

Phra Lo set out and made his way,
comely as the lion king, striding serenely from its cave.
The two women waited, watching for the arrival of the king.
They rose and went to receive him as he came, as if descending from
    the heavens to the earth. (447)

They went to him and prostrated in salute at his feet.
"We invite you, excellent and exalted king,
to the celestial pleasure abode, the royal resting place
and pleasure house of the two young royal sisters." (448)

Phra Lo replied to the ladies-in-waiting,
"The lovely princesses, are they well?" (449)

[Ruen and Roy replied,] "The two delicate princesses
have no fever but are feverish of heart, languishing in sorrow
    awaiting you, exalted lord." (450)

The king moved with stately grace and ascended the dwelling. With perfumed water from golden vessels they tenderly washed his feet, and with unblemished towels they wiped them dry. Then stepping on the cloth laid out for him, he went up onto the sleeping platform and there went to sit and rest himself. He spoke in greeting to the two women, who gestured in salutation and then spoke. "Royal lord, you are accustomed to riding elephants and horses. Palanquins wait to transport you, oh king. Beautiful carpets are spread before you, and golden slippers are placed beneath your feet. How then did you come to walk this land as a commoner, traveling along rough jungle roads? Our hearts are near breaking for you, oh burdened king." They bowed their heads in prostration to him. "How did you endure this inestimable difficulty?" (451)

The king replied to them,
"You two have compassion for me like the most solicitous of my
     royal kin. (452)

"I am determined to overcome all difficulties
because I desire to see the princesses' beautiful faces. (453)

"Be kind, and delay not.
If you love me, hasten that I might see them." (454)

[Ruen and Roy replied,] "Oh golden king, remain here and do not
     leave.
And you two attendants, watch over his highness.
We will salute and take our leave of the king.
We will fasten the lock and hide the lord, concealing him from
     sight." (455)

[Phra Lo said,] "My breast is about to burst, as you must see.
In my heart I am as one crazed!
Do not relax, but hurry and go.
Take the news to my beloved princesses. (456)

"If the two ladies desire that we see each other,
invite them to hasten here without delay.

If they are long in coming they will not see me in this life,
and I will leave behind only my royal corpse, waiting for them to
cremate my remains." (457)

The two of them saluted at his feet and then they took their leave of
him.
They instructed the two men with gentle looks.
The two pairs secretly exchanged furtive glances.
They looked and looked, and the king himself took note. (458)

The ladies went from the room, pining for their loved ones,
glancing from the corner of their eyes and sadly sending looks of
love.
The men stroked their breasts, groaning in distress.
Oh, such a separation; could any others be so burdened? (459)

They went gracefully to the outside. They fastened the golden lock
upon the gate and took the key away with them. With brimming
hearts, they hurried to go. And gracefully mounting an elephant, they
went forth. Moving quickly along the way they passed through the
great gate and neared the abode of the two princesses. Dismounting
the elephant, they entered the gate of the palace. And looking toward
the royal residence they saw the princesses in the opening of the lion
window. They were as celestial nymphs come to earth, both their faces
fresh as the orb of the moon, heavenly spheres, waiting, their gazes
fixed upon the roadway. Seeing their ladies-in-waiting, their faces
brightened as if the king himself had come. (460)

"Come, let us call out
and ask them for news so that we will have some encouragement." (461)

"But we don't want to call attention to ourselves.
It would get out to everyone, and we must not let grandmother
   know. (462)

"Oh, it would be better to kill ourselves!
Why do our two dear companions walk so slowly?" (463)

"The inner palace gates are close by, are they not?
But today it all looks different. Have they been moved farther
   away?" (464)

When the ladies-in-waiting arrived at the stairway they went up, and when they reached the floor of the palace they drew near to the princesses. They saluted their ladies and informed them of the news, telling them all in detail. They raised their hands again in salutation and said, "At this moment, your loved one has come to you, our highnesses." (465)

"Oh, our royal loved ones, great fortune is yours.
The king is as beautiful as a bar of pure gold.
He is as a divinity come to you in grandeur.
In all the world, this lord is supreme." (466)

"The king spoke, oh great royal ones, saying that
if you hurry, you shall meet with him.
But if you delay, you shall meet only with his remains.
He will have left behind only his corpse for us to cremate." (467)

[Phuean and Phaeng replied,] "Oh, a celestial jewel has descended to
   our hands.

We love him more than life. How could we wish to be separated
    from him?
But if we should be seen to hurry, the story would come out.
We must take leave of our grandmother, and then we can be quick
    to follow our hearts." (468)

The two went to their noble grandmother, and
they carefully placed her royal feet upon their heads.
They pressed close to her, resting on the dais.
They attended her with great decorum, and their grandmother was
    touched. (469)

She praised her granddaughters, exemplary young flowers.
"You two are like the newly blossomed lotus.
My grandchildren, you are filled with beauty.
Massage me and restore my strength. Oh, you care for me so
    well." (470)

She raised their faces to admire them.
"You two are so beautiful, so lovely.
So very good hearted! Who could equal you?
Your gentle touch gives me comfort and strength. (471)

"But don't force yourselves and massage me for too long.
If you try too hard in caring for me, you may fall ill.
You two ladies, Ruen and Roy, be attentive and care well for these
    princesses.
Remind them to bathe and to eat, to put on powder and to comb
    their hair." (472)

[Phuean and Phaeng replied,] "We bow in salutation at your feet.
What happiness could compare with this?
Gazing on your face, so like a lotus in bloom, we do not wish to
    depart.
It is as though heavenly oils had been brought to anoint us, making
    us forget to leave." (473)

[Their grandmother said,] "Your love for me has pleased me,
and I have listened to your clear and gentle voices.
You speak so harmoniously, whatever could compare?
It is as though some celestial potion had come to me, giving me true
    strength. (474)

"I love you and do not want you to be far from me.
If I caution you, it is because I fear that you may become ill.
I cherish you more than my own heart.
If I caution you continuously, do not be offended. (475)

"Be watchful in each of the four movements.
Reclining, sitting, standing, and walking, attend to each of these.
You two princesses, my perfect golden lotuses,
reclining, sitting, standing and walking—perfect each of them
    equally." (476)

[Phuean and Phaeng replied,] "We do not wish to be far from you,
    majesty.
Though our bodies may depart, our hearts still dwell with you.
We beg to take leave of you to go on our way,
to play among the trees and flowers of the pleasure garden." (477)

[Grandmother speaks,] "I give my leave for you to go, you two
    sisters.
Bathe in the ponds while admiring the trees and the flowers.
And when the heat of the day has passed, return again."
Hearing this, the two princesses bowed to their grandmother and
    took their leave. (478)

[Phuean and Phaeng:] "Oh, gladness beyond description!
We are to meet with the great king, and we are overjoyed." (479)

They went back to their palace and there they bathed. With powder
they adorned their faces, so like the face of the moon. Each dressed
her hair like a heavenly maiden. Each put on a skirt of the finest silk,
sparkling with the height of beauty, and a flawless sash, exquisitely
fashioned. When they were thus adorned they went forth, graceful
celestial nymphs. Their arms positioned with modesty, they walked
in grandeur to the magnificent golden mounting platform. There
they mounted a female elephant, its howdah embellished with
elegant carvings and its precious saddle adorned with the forms of
graceful animals. The elephant was dazzling to the eye, with regalia
of glittering beauty. (480)

Following them in a grand procession came shimmering banners and
parasols of golden peacock feathers, beautifully decorated jeweled
umbrellas, palm-leaf fans, and hair whisks, and numerous maidens
of high rank. The noble ladies-in-waiting followed the princesses, and
they quickly reached the gate of the royal park. A golden palanquin
received the princesses and bore them gracefully to the dwelling
within. The ladies-in-waiting, with attentive haste, went before them
and unlocked the door. As for the king, with great care he had donned

his crown and raiment, his incomparable garments and jewelry. Beautiful as Indra descended from the heavens, he concealed himself within the jeweled dwelling, awaiting the embrace of his two beloved ones. (481)

His two attendants also concealed themselves at the sides of the dais. Ruen hurried to cover the seat in preparation for the appearance of the two princesses. Outside, in accordance with custom, the servants and the members of the retinue waited in attendance. Roy, speaking deferentially, said, "Your royal grandmother directed us to be diligent in reminding you to take to your rest." And the two princesses replied, in pretense, "Soon enough, we shall recline." Ruen raised her arms in salute and said, "Your royal grandmother gave instructions in all matters, as the ladies of your retinue will bear witnesses. Though we might quickly forget her words, they would remember and we would be flogged." Roy then hastened to pull open the curtains and invited the two exalted ones to enter. "As for you, oh lady retainers, so long as you remain, the princesses will not sleep. So, go down now and seek diversion among the trees, and admire the flowers and the vines. Only the two of us need remain behind to attend the princesses." And when the body of retainers had made their exit, the ladies-in-waiting closed every door. (482)

And then they
bowed in salutation and invited the delicate ones to go inside. (483)

Their hearts had been like a cloudless sky,
but hearing this invitation, they were slow to comply; timidly, they
hesitated. (484)

[Phuean and Phaeng said,] "Oh, throughout all our lives
we have acquired no experience, not even a bit.
How can we go in this way? We beg you to tell us how we should
begin.
Our apprehension mounts, and in truth we are afraid." (485)

[Ruen and Roy replied,] "Your highnesses, you are not children.
Even those with no experience must first begin, and then they will
know.
Oh, our dear princesses, do not hold back.
Have you no feeling for the king?" (486)

Phra Lo, concealed behind the curtain, came close to listen.
Hearing their hidden thoughts, he realized that they truly were still
young.
He sat close to the princesses' backs,
but they were unaware and continued speaking with their ladies-in-
waiting. (487)

[Phuean and Phaeng continued,] "Oh, we love the king more than
our own hearts.
We have never known this kind of pain.
We are troubled and wish we could quickly gain experience.
We beg you, teach us these arts so that we can master them." (488)

Hearing this, Ruen and Roy smiled in amusement.
"Who could teach you such things?
On the day that you first loved and longed for the king,
who taught you how to weep and sob and moan?" (489)

[Phuean and Phaeng replied,] "Well, if you won't teach us, at least
   don't ridicule us!

Don't be so unfeeling toward us!

You first looked upon the sun and the moon, the day and the night,
   long before we did.

We ask because we don't know of these things. If we did know,
   would we ask?" (490)

[Ruen and Roy replied,] "Oh princesses, how could we tell you?

You will understand fully once you are in the king's presence.

It won't take long. There is nothing to be concerned about!

In just a short time you will master these arts all on your own." (491)

Phra Lo could no longer restrain himself, and he laughed.

The two princesses were frightened and started.

With his royal face like a lotus in bloom, and close to the two of
   them,

he pulled back the silken curtain, allowing them to cast their eyes
   upon him. (492)

And so, they looked upon the king,

magnificent as the sun, a celestial jewel.

Forgetting their embarrassment, they now forgot themselves and
   met the king's gaze.

They looked upon him unblinking, thinking, "Oh, this must be a
   god." (493)

When they had regained control, they looked at each other in
   consternation.

And then they prostrated in respectful greeting.

Their appearance pleased both the eye and heart of the king.

Looking to the older and then to the younger, the king, in turn, forgot himself. (494)

"Are these golden lotuses plucked from the water?

Or stars descended from the skies?

Or has the moon quit the heavens to come to me?

Enraptured, I look upon these enchanting young faces." (495)

The princesses gazed upon the king and ceased not in their gazing.

The great king gazed upon the faces of the princesses,

and sitting close by them he ceased not in his gazing.

The princesses bowed in salutation at his feet; they bowed, and they bowed again. (496)

Roy and Ruen also performed their salutation and looked upon the king.

They then looked upon the princesses, close to him in attendance.

Gazing upon the ladies, they forgot the king.

Gazing upon the king, they forgot the ladies. (497)

They gazed upon the king: "This noble one is the sun."

They gazed upon the princesses: "They are the moon in a clear sky."

They gazed in wonder: "What has come about here?

Have the moon and the sun appeared to visit with each other?" (498)

[Ruen said,] "Mistress Roy, I beg you to observe this carefully.

We know that our princesses are lovely beyond all others.

But the appearance of the king has enhanced their beauty.

All the divinities have combined their skills to create these three." (499)

[Roy replied,] "Cast your gaze upon them. One cannot cease in
    looking.
Throughout all the three realms can any be found to compare?
We must in truth have great merit, my dear Ruen,
that we see these three royal meritorious ones." (500)

"You two men, where are you, dear ones?
Come and help us to gaze upon these exalted faces,
our hearts' fulfillment, transcending all the world,
these three royal highnesses of befitting beauty." (501)

The two women praised them without ceasing. And the two men,
both thoroughly versed, knelt and entered. At a deferential distance,
they prostrated themselves at the feet of the king and the princesses,
straightening their fingers and bringing their hands together in
respectful obeisance. They admired the appearance of all three,
whose beauty arrested the eye and captivated the heart. In all the
kingdoms beneath the skies they saw only these three, the royal king
and princesses. (502)

[Kaew and Khwan:] "Timeless, surpassing beauty, all the work of
    gods.
Their graceful forms draw to them the eyes of all the earth.
Most fitting, most satisfying.
More lovely than lovely. Oh, they gladden the heart." (503)

The four attendants saluted the three royal ones.
"Wipe your golden lotus feet, highnesses,
and go to take your rest. Sleep, oh royal ones,
lest the three of you be weary." (504)

Phra Lo shook the sky and the earth with his graceful step.
The two princesses followed this ruler of the three realms.
The three of them raised their arms and faces in a beautiful manner.
They were as the risen moon and stars, casting their light upon the
  heavens and the earth. (505)

Roy and Ruen washed the dust from the feet of the royal ones,
Wiping the feet of the three, most high.
They then invited them to enter the bedchamber,
And attend them as would heavenly maidens. (506)

Closing the curtain, they invoked the spirits of the exalted ones.
"Oh be not far from the princesses.
Be for them as encircling vines.
Be for the king as the trunk of a golden tree, enticing the vines to
  encircle it." (507)

They then took leave of the royal ones, bowing low at their feet.
When they reached the outside, they shut the gates.
And with the gates shut, they went directly to the men.
Even sitting apart, the passion of these lovers seared them as would
  a consuming fire. (508)

They held in check the inflamed passion of their desires.
Driven by loyal constancy, they restrained the yearnings of their
  hearts. (509)

Mindful of their duties, they felt troubled.
If they had not been mindful they would not have felt
  constrained. (510)

[The attendants conversed:]

"This dwelling is a pleasing place for sporting,

and though we deplore the idea, we do want to play. But would it not

be shameful?" (511)[149]

"All would criticize us behind our backs.

If we ignored them and acted on our desires, would we not be

misbehaving?" (512)

"First love is fueled with passion, impatient for the beloved,

more powerful than tongues of flame in a consuming conflagration.

The royal dwelling of these great rulers is a place of propriety.

We constrain ourselves because of our loyalty." (513)

"We are all their devoted intimates.

We hate and fear even a speck of wrongdoing.

If the weight of a misdeed equaled that of even half a strand of hair,

we would die,

For that would be better than being faulted from behind our

backs." (514)

The four of them considered these words favorably.

They counseled each other quietly and so cooled the hot fires of

their passion. (515)

As for the royal ones,

They embraced, drawing themselves to each other, joyfully pressing

together. (516)

In joyful admiration of each other

they tasted the nectar of a kiss, caressing in tumultuous love. (517)

Arm intertwined with arm in loving embrace.
Flesh pressed to lovely flesh, doing the bidding of their hearts. (518)

Clear visages, fresh faces.
Faces pressed to faces, youthful faces of great beauty. (519)

Breasts pressed against breasts, supple and young.
Midriff pressed against midriff, in mutual arousal. (520)

They united in intoxicating love.
Mixing flavors, mixing scents, mixing in sensuality, mixing in
    passion. (521)

The lotus blossoms opened,
flower upon flower, overlaying flower, probing the royal lotus
    pond. (522)

The bee fondled its mate
in the middle of the lotus, and grasping they called out in shared
    provocation. (523)

Bathing in a celestial pond could not have been its equal.
The ponds of the royal women, smooth of skin, provided an
    enchanting bath. (524)

Pleasure in the young ones' ponds,
Delighted, the fish sprang up to touch the opened lotus blossom. (525)

How enticing were the banks of these precious ponds.
Clear as though swept clean, no celestial mound could compare. (526)

Great merit brought the king to come
admire the princesses' golden breasts. "Oh, I beg to admire them." (527)

Regal Phuean having united with her love's desire,
King Lo turned to admire the precious one, essence of nobility, the
golden Phaeng. (528)

And again, he indulged in wondrous pleasures.
Without fatigue, without pausing, the bold lover united with his
loved one. (529)

As a steed enflamed by the five cravings,
driven by consuming passion, he did not slacken. (530)

As an elephant wild with intoxicating rut,
with thrusting, stabbing tusks and grasping trunk, he joined her in
mutual seeking. (531)

He caressed the princesses.
"Oh, my precious ones, I have experienced great difficulty for your
sake. (532)

"Have pity and do not resist me.
Please princesses, young and supple, be kind and bear with me." (533)

[Phuean and Phaeng replied,] "Oh royal one, virtuous beyond
reckoning,

Oh great king, have pity on us.

We are completely innocent of these things.

Care for and be gentle with us, oh meritorious one!" (534)

[Phra Lo replied,] "Have no concern, my ladies.

I love you more than the earth, more than the sky.

I will protect you to the end, more even than myself.

If we were separated for only a single watch, then I would die."[150] (535)

His lovemaking did not lessen but increased.

The princesses languished in their fatigue.

Lovemaking is like a heavenly bath that cleanses and enlivens.

Now fortified, now weary, but when the weariness has passed,

   contented. (536)

The sound of thunder reverberated throughout the heavens.

The earth was left limp and shrank back.

Great waves stirred the sea, and the ocean turned to foam.

And in every direction the trees swayed wondrously.[151] (537)

The lion king caressed his mate, the lion queen.

The bull elephant pressed against the elephant cow, seeking pleasure.

The golden deer stalked its loved one in joyful play.

The rabbits and squirrels danced about, joining their partners in

   lovemaking. (538)

The sun rose above the trees,[152] gazing down upon the lotus.

The lotus would not open, fearing the repeated striking of the bee.

The bee, intoxicated, pressed in upon the lotus,

   immersing itself within the petals, wallowing in their pollen. (539)

It did not withdraw or relent in any way.
Driven by desire to continue the struggle, it did not desist.
Oh, pity the lotus blossom, with no relief,
Unwilling to open, unlike the other blossoms. (540)

The sun approached the boundaries of the sky
and the two ladies-in-waiting said, "Oh royal ones, darkness
    approaches." (541)

The king spread the curtains
and called the four attendants to enter. (542)

He considered all in his heart and then instructed them,
"Conceal this secret and let no one see the ruse." (543)

Immediately saluting the king,
they accepted his royal command and then spoke. (544)

"We invite you to bathe and so cool yourself.
Go to the golden basin and cleanse yourself together with the
    princesses." (545)

The lotus pressed in among the flowers,
touching them playfully, and they were refreshed. (546)

From the bath, he proceeded to the jeweled dais
and, donning his beautiful raiment, sat embracing them. (547)

The ladies-in-waiting bowed their heads
and brought forth the foods that they had prepared. (548)

The princesses gestured in respect
and prompted him, saying, "Noble king,[153] we invite you to eat." (549)

He raised their chins and admired their oval[154] faces.
"I invite you both to eat along with me. (550)

"Heavenly edibles could not compare to these
because, as I eat, you are pressed close to me. (551)

"Oh my young loved ones, the food you place in my mouth
has a heavenly flavor, stirring my passion and my feelings for
     you." (552)

When they had eaten to their hearts content,
the ladies-in-waiting saluted the royal ones and reminded them, (553)

"The sun is approaching the edge of the sky.
Great king, do not delay. Princesses, the time has come." (554)

[Phra Lo said,] "Oh young ones, do not so willingly depart from me.
I gaze upon you and I weep."
The three of them were despondent in their love.
Faces pressed together, they shed a stream of tears. (555)

Oh pity the two lovely young royals,
bending to his lap in a respectful obeisance.
Tears bathed their faces, pouring down in a flood.
They cried out endlessly, sobbing in pain. (556)

"Oh pinnacle of the earthly realm,

from the first, when we began to hear news of you,
we were unable to eat but languished in desire for you.
We could not sleep and lay feverish with love, waiting for word of
    you. (557)

"We sought help from all the divinities of the great mountains
and even the tree-dwelling spirits of the woodlands,
asking that they help bring you to unite with us,
promising that afterward we would venerate them all. (558)

"Silver and gold and mounds of gems we promised them,
and elephants, tusks decorated with gold, and albino buffalo.
Our ardent supplications seeking satisfaction were successful.
Had we not united with you, we would never have known a
    husband's love. (559)

"And so, you made your way here to be with us.
Yet after not even a day of love our separation is upon us.
How can we be parted in this way?"
They embraced the king, weeping in their hunger for him. (560)

Equally afflicted, the king was heartsick.
He hid his royal face and sighed.
Leaning over the princesses, perfect golden lotus blossoms,
he did not want to turn his gaze away from his loved ones. (561)

"I have tasted happiness as if I were the great Indra.
From the very first that I heard news of you,
if I could fly I would have flown to you young women.

But I could not come, and my passion was restrained as though
    imprisoned. (562)

"Forsaking my broad city and my elephants and steeds,
I left behind my mother and my wife to come to you.
I left behind my concubines, beautiful as flowers in a bouquet.
I came alone, and now I am bound together with you. (563)

"I have been with you for only a single watch,
and yet we are as a cord of three strands, meticulously plaited.
Will you now turn away so quickly and leave me?
Should you ladies depart, I would be overwhelmed and die. (564)

"Or do you love me not and so are leaving me?
If you did love me would you be able to go?
Solitary and alone I made my way here from afar.
Yet you are going to forsake me, abandoned and alone." (565)

They heard the words of the great king as a searing hot fire that
    would not abate.
"Come, we shall beat ourselves, even to the point of death.
Oh, how can you say that we sever our hearts' connections with you?
We do not wish to be separated from you, even by the width of
    strand of hair." (566)

Thus the two princesses replied to him.
And the sun, passing through the sky, descended.
Ruen and Roy reminded the princesses, "It will soon be dark.
When darkness comes there will be much talk, and that will bring
    trouble." (567)

They saluted the three royal ones and said, "Oh, it won't be long.
You will be separated for only a moment's time—at nightfall you
     will reunite. (568)

"Oh, great and handsome king,
please bid the princesses go." (569)

In sadness the king then gently said,
"Please, young ladies, go gracefully forth." (570)

The two princesses prostrated in salute.
He lifted their faces and kissed them farewell. (571)

Their faces were melancholy, burning with passion.
They saluted at his feet, sighing and weeping, and slowly made their
     way. (572)

They turned back frequently.
Oh so sad, these young ones replied to the lord in this way: (573)

"May it not be long, your highness.
Oh exalted king, hasten our reuniting." (574)

[Phra Lo replied,] "I ache more than I can say.
I wish to go along with you. Separation from you is like death." (575)

The ladies-in-waiting made gestures of respect and invited the
princesses to the mounting platform, where they were received by
the sound of golden conch shells and by the numerous lady retainers.
Ruen, skilled in the art of deception, hid their stratagem completely.

Having closed the doors, she followed the princesses to the gate and then pretended that she had forgotten some regalia within the bejeweled sleeping chamber. "Come, dear Roy, I will go look. You will have to hold open the door and wait for me." They went without delay to the dwelling of happiness, the celestial abode, and unlocked the royal portal. Leaving Roy on watch, Ruen went in to escort the king, and the two men followed gracefully behind.[155] And so, in the darkness of nightfall, when their faces could not be seen, the great king and his attendants went out in disguise. (576)

> Reaching the inner gate of the royal residence
> they made their way toward the princesses' abode.
> They invited the king to ascend into the dwelling
> and to stay in hiding in Roy's chambers. (577)

> Both ladies-in-waiting accompanied him,
> And they also concealed his two attendants, keeping them from
>   sight. (578)

> When the darkness of night had obscured the sky
> they invited the king to ascend in secret to reunite with the
>   princesses. (579)

> The princesses, adorable as flower blossoms,
> came out to receive the king, and he went in. (580)

> "Oh king, why were you so long in arriving?
> Would you have left us to die of grief?" (581)

> They held out their hands to lead him

to ascend to the heavenly dais, and they were enraptured. (582)

The handsome king placed himself
upon the silken mat and precious cushions that the princesses had
    prepared for him. (583)

The sparkling curtains were of surpassing quality,
with rings of the finest copper and gold, all with golden inlay. (584)

Flowers were plaited into dense garlands,
and the blossoms bathed the sleeping chamber with fragrance. (585)

In the ceiling were numerous gems,
the beauty of gold alternating with their glimmering luster, beauty
    to surround the princesses. (586)

They presented him with royal garments, all valuable as gold.
They presented him with fragrant powders[156] with which to anoint
    his body.
They presented him with a betel nut tray carved with the *mangkon*
    and studded with gems.
The delicate ladies carefully presented royal foods for the king's
    consumption. (587)

Having partaken of food, the three partook of pleasure.
Having shut the golden doors of the sleeping chamber,
the two ladies-in-waiting went to unite with the king's two
    attendants.
They laughed in continual pleasure, caressing and embracing their
    loved ones. (588)

The two women contrived to conceal the king.
Only these two ladies-in-waiting knew.
About half of a month passed gradually by,
and they took great pleasure from their play, knowing no fading of
   their desire. (589)

[Meanwhile, to others] they appeared at times feverish, at times
joyously happy. At times, they were relaxed and playful. At times, they
hid themselves from sight, whispering secretively. Only the ladies-
in-waiting went inside, and all others were forbidden. All the large
retinue, of every rank, nudged each other and furtively said, "All this
is truly strange. Our two princesses and their ladies-in-waiting are
concealing something!" (590)

But, like the smoke of a fire, it leaked out and was known.
One person saw and nudged another to look. (591)

All pretended neither to see nor to hear.
They feigned disinterest and ignorance.
But the news did spread and reached the king,
the father of the princesses. (592)

He came, also in stealth, to observe his children,
and his rage was as scorching lightning in parched grass, spreading
   conflagration. (593)

Secretly he watched.
But King Lo was so beautiful that his fury abated. (594)

[King Phichaiphitsanukon thought,] "Perhaps their merit has
brought this about.
Though once kept far apart they are now together, as if by a
miracle." (595)

Secretly he admired Phra Lo.
"This King Lo is the equal of a hundred who already feel the weight
of our foot. (596)

"Taking him would be like
the sky and the earth come to be in our grasp. (597)

"[And] accepting him as a beloved son-in-law
would bring honor without end, and value beyond all
estimation." (598)

The king then made his presence known, and the princesses saluted at
his feet. The royal King Lo inquired, and the princesses told him the
name of their father. King Lo then raised his hands in salute. Offering
pleasing gestures of respect, he bowed in obeisance and spoke, saying,
"Royal king, I abandoned my own royal treasure, and having set it
aside, I have come here alone to find you. Royal father and king, I
ask to join your lineage to be of the same noble line, a member of
the same royal family until the end of time." The king heard these
words and his heart opened like a blossoming lotus. His handsome
face shone as brightly as that of an emperor. He had obtained a great
king as an ally, as the first among his royal offspring together with
the royal princesses. "An auspicious month and day shall be selected,
and then will I arrange for a ceremony of marriage." Having spoken,
the king returned to his royal residence. This news spread, reaching

the princesses' grandmother, and she went to him to plead, "Oh king and ruler, the child of our most wicked enemy, your father's murderer, has come in secret to dishonor you, shaming your daughters, my grandchildren, and you are going to permit him to do it! Spare him not! Slay your enemy! We should have him slashed to pieces. We should have him cut and flayed, piece by piece, until we are sated." But no matter how she pleaded, the king paid no heed. So she went to her own palace and addressed the boldest of her fighting men, her most skilled and senior servants, saying falsely, "Our exalted king has entrusted this responsibility to us. I want all of you, each one, to kill this man who so disdains and scorns us. But hold our plan in the deepest of secrecy, hidden completely from all others. Whosoever shall reveal our secret, punish him to the highest degree. Slit his throat and so let him perish, because he had no respect for my words." They took upon themselves these royal orders and declared their willingness to fight: "Let our lady wait and observe the strategy that we shall employ." They prepared themselves in secret, and when the night was darkest and all in a hush, they surrounded the chambers of the princesses, encircling all the area three deep, blocking it to all and allowing no one to enter or to leave. But Kaew and Khwan were told of this, and they made straight for their king and told him of this secret plan. The king smiled brightly and laughed. He felt no fear but instead was even more ennobled, and with the bearing of the great lion king he brandished his weapons. As for Kaew and Khwan, they declared their readiness to their lord. "With clear hearts, we beg that we may precede you in death." The two princesses prostrated in consternation at his feet. The lord consoled them, saying, "You two adored ones, do not be fearful; this is of no consequence." And he encouraged them to smile and laugh joyfully. And so, the two ladies were gladdened and without delay regained their composure. "We too are of royal blood. We are not cowards, nor are we fearful of death. We shall have no other man as our mate. Nor shall we live only to have people cast ridicule upon us, or to have even our servants look down upon us. When you return to the gods in the heavenly city, we shall follow after you in death. Oh king, be not concerned for us!" Wrapping their shawls in layers around themselves and binding up their soft clothing, they brandished swords and placed themselves beside their monarch. And with no delay, Roy and Ruen grew glad at heart and certain in their course of action. "If the three royal ones should go to the heavens, who then shall we serve? Who would ever have respect for us? May we then perish along with the royal ones and live with them in the city on high, preserving our dignity for others to praise." First gesturing in respect to the king, the two then disguised themselves as men. And so, dressed in men's garments and strutting about with swords raised high, Ruen went to be with Kaew on the right and Roy came quickly to be with Khwan on the left, allowing for no separation between them. Seeing this marvel, the great king positioned himself in the center with the two ladies pressed against him on either side, and the king and the princesses kissed. The two men drew close to the two ladies-in-waiting, embracing them with admiration and praise. Before long the grandmother's men reached the gates of the palace. Kaew struck and slashed with his sword, and Khwan stabbed at them with all his might. And swordsmen were defeated and fled. Blows were exchanged thick and fast. The king pushed forward, slashing and cutting. The dead fell upon each other, collapsing together in great heaps. The attackers hurriedly hurled in rocks and stones and rushed in, advancing in a body, and with the trunks of trees they broke down the walls. And the two attendants moved about wildly, repelling them like crazed elephants in rut. (599)

They moved into the center of the fray, avoiding the arrows, not allowing themselves to be struck, and evading the spears, not letting themselves be pierced. The attackers unleashed volleys of arrows into the confusion. Together they hurled spears from all sides. On the left, they pressed forward in masses. On the right, they pressed forward in multitudes. They came in through every opening, crowding together into the fight. The two men rushed forward slashing at them in all directions, knocking away their protective charms and severing their heads. The attackers fired in arrows like a flood, piercing Kaew mortally and striking Khwan, who both collapsed in death. Ruen then pressed into the battle, slashing at them, and Roy attacked, stabbing and thrusting with the point of her sword. Not realizing that these were women, the attackers fired and hit the two of them, who fell toward the corpses of their husbands, hurling themselves atop the bodies of the two men, and so the four of them perished together. The lord looked upon his attendants and praised them greatly. "They are all most deserving of love. How could we fail to follow their example?" And then the princesses called out in laughter. "The four of them did not fear destruction. Could we, then, both of royal blood, fear death and thus invite never-ending shame? Whether we are to perish or escape, we will be with you, oh king, and will not move from you. (600)

"Oh dear king, royal highness, have no doubt.
We would die rather than be separated from you.
Be not concerned over whether you will live.
When could you expect to have a death like this one? (601)

"After death we will be born again, together,
to rule a heavenly kingdom in the far reaches of the sky.

We would not choose to live only to be mocked by others, royal one.
And living without seeing your face would be as death itself. (602)

"We have yet to begin to fight, and yet the four of them have already
   perished.
We two, of royal pedigree, will not separate ourselves from you.
We do love ourselves but are fearful of a terrible disgrace.
We love you and if we can die with you, how could we choose to go
   on living?" (603)

Having heard the princesses,
   the king laughed heartily and smiled at them with delight. (604)

The two royal princesses,
   braver than brave and bolder than bold, feared only disgrace. (605)

Not burdened by fear of death, even so much as the weight of a
   strand of hair,
   they clutched their swords and advanced upon their enemies. (606)

Engaging the enemy, they slashed and cut them, and turning, stabbed
them. With violent swings of the sword they severed their heads and
limbs, all three magnificent, grand as the lion king. Brandishing their
weapons with bold authority, they had no fear. They smiled broadly
and laughed, and extending their arms they made war all about them,
intimidating all, in every direction. The attackers pressed in on all
sides, but they were consumed like armloads of straw thrown upon
a fire. So others did not come in close but gathered at a distance
to fire upon the three royal ones, who used their swords to knock
the arrows aside. Then the attackers fired in many more arrows, too

many to repel, and so struck the king. The two beautiful princesses were not fearful. Shielding the king with their own bodies they, too, were hit. Poisoned arrows poured in on them, and they were pierced everywhere, shedding their royal blood. The three of them leaned against each other, their faces turned toward their enemies, as though purposefully arrayed. Arriving together at life's end, they stood as though still alive. All the attackers were now struck with fear. The news spread unchecked and reached Lord Phitsanukon, who came in haste. He saw his two beloved daughters and the magnificent King Lo, their bodies bathed in blood, standing together as if they had not yet perished. Brushing back his constant tears he called out to his noble daughters and beloved son-in-law. But no matter how he called to them, they did not speak. No matter how he touched them, they did not move. They stood, leaning stiffly against one another. And then the king knew well that the three of them had met their fate. Feigning satisfaction instead of ire, he proclaimed, "The guilty have all been dispatched, following each other in death, and I am satisfied. But who was bold and clever enough to destroy them? Let them now come forward to claim their prize. Whoever these brave and daring ones may be, they will reap rewards beyond their expectation. I will grant them the rank of *khun*, with rewards of one thousand and ten thousand." So they were sought out and brought before him, without delay and without exception. And he bade them be bound about the neck with ropes and their elbows tied together with fiber and their legs pierced with spears. And their names were taken down, each one, to the last man, and then their bodies were sliced as one slices the trunk of a banana tree.[157] Swords cut them, and writhing in agony they died. He ordered their officers boiled and burned alive. And the old grandmother he had flayed, and declaring, "You are not my mother!" he had her killed most painfully. And when their corpses had been dragged away he returned to his noble offspring and sobbed ceaselessly, "Oh, my precious children! (607)

"Oh each of you celestial beauties,
what suffering it is to look upon your faces, now lost to me. (608)

"Come, let me join you in death.
My pain knows no bounds. How can I live this way? (609)

"My heart is overwhelmed.
Oh precious daughters, my suffering is beyond measure." (610)

And revered Darawadi, royal queen and mother, received the news. Her heart raced and she collapsed, hiding her face in grief. She fell into confusion, her breast trembling. Her retinue tended to their queen and with their help she mounted her palanquin. They followed behind her in all their great numbers, each one in tears. She arrived at the princesses' abode, weakened and distracted, languishing like a fallen golden vine, her tears cascading down in a flood. They raised her palanquin up to the floor of the royal dwelling, and there she saw the three royal ones, come to the end of their lives. She threw herself down, striking her breast, and rolled about on the floor. "I have come to see you, precious children. What is this anger you show me? You will not speak to me. You have not made up your faces for me to gaze upon, nor have you combed your hair for me to admire. You will not lift your faces for my kiss. You have not perfumed your bodies with flower water, nor applied the fragrant civet powder.[158] You have not partaken of your meal, and yet you make your way to the heavens, leaving me here, bereft! Oh my ladies, have pity on me, your mother! (611)

"Why does it please you to hasten onto death?
Open your mouths and speak with me, that I may be glad. (612)

"What has displeased you so?
Should you be so angry that you take yourselves to the heavens? (613)

"What distress speeds you on your away?
Be not angry with me, oh my loved ones! (614)

"Oh, see the dim light of the early morning.
Go and cleanse your teeth, my ladies. (615)

"Go down to relieve yourselves, my dears,
and when you return then bathe. (616)

"Put on your royal adornments and fan your faces.
Put on your clothes and your girdle and then walk gracefully here to
    see me. (617)

"Come, you two, and prepare flower arrangements,
and offer incense and candles and gold at the royal feet of the
    Buddha.[159] (618)

"And then come, ladies.
Come and eat with me, oh my dearest ones." (619)

Thus she prompted them, but they gave no response. She touched
them, but they did not move. They only stood, leaning stiffly against
one another. "Oh, has King Lo forbidden you to reply? (620)

"His royal highness,
your father, has come to visit with you, and you will not look upon
   him? (621)

"And now you will not turn your faces to me.
Have you not a single word for your mother? (622)

"What shall I do with this fruitless life?
Though I may live, madness shall be my companion.
If I cannot be with my own children, I would be better off dead.
For if I were to die would I not immediately see their faces?" (623)

Every member of the royal family wept loudly.
Every one of the royal concubines fell into tears.
From the ladies of the palace down even to the common people of
   the city,
not one person was able to keep from rolling about upon the
   ground. (624)

The sound of weeping came from every subject, from every
   household.
The entire kingdom was overwhelmed by grief.[160]

They did not see the sun, the moon, or the stars, and for them all
   was dark and dim.
Wherever one looked there was water, the water of peoples' tears. (625)

The king and all the women of his household
cried out in pain and sorrow, and their tears were mixed with
   blood. (626)

But with great discernment
the king determined to control his heart, and so he regained his
    composure. (627)

The weeping of the rulers slackened.
And the two of them forbade all the others from further crying. (628)

When the sound of weeping abated,
they praised the three valiant-hearted ones. (629)

"How admirable they were to have perished thus, standing
    together.[161]
We know they had truly royal hearts, beyond equal. (630)

"And King Lo's two attendants,
and Ruen and Roy, are like incomparable divinities. (631)

"Bold hearts, to die before their lord and ladies,
companions embracing in death, couples so deserving of love." (632)

Everyone in the land
spoke in admiration, filling the city with their praises. (633)

The earth echoed with their fame,
and the sky resounded with the melodious sound, calling them to
    the heavens. (634)

Even the great oceans cried out boisterously. Every district of the
capital city was beset by fever. His majesty Lord Phichaiphitsanukon
ordered the beautiful Darawadi escorted back to her dwelling, and

then he bade them bathe the corpses of the three royal ones, arrange
the various adornments, and wrap the bodies. They carefully erected
a great golden casket and in it placed all three. And then he bade them
prepare another casket in which to place Khun Kaew[162] and Lady
Ruen, and yet another for Muen Khwan and Lady Roy. When all had
been done according to funereal custom, he set out for the palace.
He bade that royal artisans be brought to him, to whom he gave
orders to construct the royal *meru*,[163] with assignments stipulated
for each department. He had them prepare a ceremonial mountain
for each of the eight directions, and royal balustrades, parasols,
tiered umbrellas, flags and banners, and many wonderful *butsabok*[164]
decorated with designs of birds and swans, lifelike[165] and carefully
crafted. Images of horses were harnessed to some of the mountains.
Some were harnessed to sparkling *mangkon* adorned with drivers
and coachmen for the vehicles. Some were adorned with images of
elephants, others with those of *khotchasi*.[166] Steadfast charioteers held
the reins and with graceful arms grasped their weapons, striking
bold poses. With splendid leaps they drove the elephants and lions.
Some were harnessed to a bullock standing upon a mountaintop.[167]
All were arranged in proper order. Also depicted were giants and
garuda, humans and *naga* and titans, all arranged in neat order. They
expanded the hall for performance and dance. They erected towers
for fireworks in rows, like candles. Revolving lamps and lens lamps
were made, and lanterns beautifully carved were hung from tall poles.
The lofty lampposts were arranged in rows. They raised posts as high
as the walls and put up a royal enclosure with lamps to pay homage
to the corpses of the three royal ones. And he gave orders to bring
ambassadors and emissaries to him, and he bade them memorize the
words of his royal message.[168] He also ordered all manner of gifts to
be taken and laid at the feet of the noble Bunluea, regal queen mother

of the family of the sun.[169] She listened to all the words of the message, and she was unable to remain standing. The noble one bowed her head in grief and collapsed onto pillows. Her hands hiding her face, she wept, sobbing constantly for the love for her noble child. She wept unceasingly, "Oh, my precious child. (635)

"I feared that it would be this way.
I forbade you, dear one, countless times, but you did not listen to
    me." (636)

"I had hoped that when your death came, whether by fever or by spirits, it would be here in our own city. I could have cared for you to my heart's content. Why did you have to go to perish in their city, by their spears, sabers, lances, and swords, by their arrows bathed in poison? (637)

"I cared for you from the moment you were conceived
and never relaxed my guard, not even for a moment,
until the time of your ascension to the throne of the kingdom.
I loved you, my child, a hundred times more than I loved myself. (638)

"You were no ordinary ruler, my child.
You were a supreme monarch, above all others.
Rulers of countless cities[170] came to pay you respect,
laying tribute at your feet nearly every day. (639)

"You took your pleasures in a heavenly palace, my child.
When you appeared in your audience hall, royalty crowded about in
    attendance.

Heads of cities, *muen*, and *khun*, assembled in haste with nobles,
   freemen, and soldiers,
All at your feet, oh companion to Indra. (640)

"Your elephants equaled those of the immortal Indra.
Your horses were like the steeds of the sun, descended from the skies.
Your numerous troops and soldiers filled the earth in happiness.
This city of yours, ruler of the earth, was like a city in the
   heavens. (641)

"What karma has deluded you?" She wept with love for her royal
son. Lamentation shaking her entire body, she seemed close to death.
Oh pity the royal queen, Laksanawadi, when she heard. She hurried
to her highness, the queen mother, along with her retinue and the
royal concubines, companions to the king. All of them came—and
none stayed behind—to the residence of the exalted noble. Seeing
her in tears, she asked, "What causes you such grief?" When she
heard the reply, she struck and beat her breast and pulled at her hair,
releasing it, unkempt, and threw herself down, weeping and calling
out imploringly, echoing throughout the palace. Hearing the forlorn
weeping, the city was crazed, as though it would collapse. Throughout
the kingdom, everyone wept, lamenting their beloved lord as if they
themselves were near death. (642)

They wept without ceasing,
   as though they would all die with their lord. (643)

The aged counselors
   urged the lord's retinue to endure: "Cease your weeping and
      consider the situation. (644)

"Do you not see that the kingdom is endangered?
Consider this most carefully, each one of you." (645)

They attended the queen and
prostrating in salutation made their report to her. (646)

"What has come to pass brings fear for the kingdom.
Majesty, think of what is to come now that the king has met his
  fate. (647)

"If we misstep, the kingdom will be destroyed.
The ghosts and even our household spirits will but wait to
  overthrow us. (648)

"Consider carefully before you respond.
Please do not err in even the slightest way, so that we may know
  success." (649)

They saluted her again, saying,
"Think most carefully royal lady—attend to all these matters." (650)

The queen listened, and she thanked her counselors.
"I would like to go myself to consign my beloved son's remains to
  the flames.
But I fear for the city, lest there be those who speak badly of us.
I would rather die and have it over with, so no one could even look
  upon me. (651)

"Hasten to bring me people who are familiar with such matters,
clever of mind and exact and eloquent of speech.

Bring ten of great *khun* rank. Let them not delay but quickly prepare
  themselves,
And prepare a hundredweight of silver and a hundredweight of gold
  for them to take. (652)

"Gather all of the nine gems, and cloth of radiant hue,
each in great quantities, and do so quickly.
Then select only the fleetest of elephants and horses, and with
  soldiers,
go in my place to manage the last affairs of my son and lord. (653)

"Present these gifts to the king of Song
and to the royal mother of the two princesses.
Write my message on palm leaves made of gold, and then hasten on
  your way.
Preserve all that is good and do not allow bad reports to come back
  to us." (654)

"When they have attended to the corpse of the great king, ask to
  receive
ashes of the three royal ones and their attendants.
When you take your leave, do so with respect, and then come here
  with circumspection.
Compose your statements with polished words and bring no shame
  upon us." (655)

The queen then granted permission for the visitors to attend her
and take their leave. She presented them with gifts, and when all was
completed she hastened the preparation of her own emissary. And
they too soon set out, and upon arrival they presented her message

of salutation and the items to be used in adorning the corpses. The king of Song agreed to all their requests. When the preparation of the corpses was complete he committed them to the flames. And then there was as a great festival, with the sounds of music everywhere, the joyful resounding of gongs and drums and the melodious harmonies of conch horns. All joined in a reverberating chorus of sound that shook the surface of the earth as though lightning had struck the ground and the sea were in a tumult. The lamps were radiant, brilliant beyond what the eye can behold. Everywhere was shimmering beauty, and steady brilliance blazed brightly. Everything was beautiful, down to the last detail. And when all the festivities were finished, His majesty provided a set of decorated vessels to receive the ashes. He had them divide the ashes of the three royals into two portions. One half he reserved in the hall of his royal family, and the other half he gave over to his visitors. He ordered that the route be decorated beautifully all the way to the far reaches of his territory, and he ordered that the ashes be carried in procession. As for her majesty Queen Bunluea, she ordered the preparation of a great vehicle to receive the royal ashes and carry them back into her great royal capital, her expansive celestial city. She prepared a palace with a pinnacled roof and there carefully placed the ashes of the three royals. And on each side, to the right and left, she built regal dwellings—on the right for Khun Kaew and Lady Ruen, and on the left for Muen Khwan and Lady Roy. The lady did all wholeheartedly, with great and surpassing beauty. She attended to all preparations both large and small, to present alms to the great triple gem for the benefit of the great king. She opened the treasury to give alms throughout the land, and everyone received them. And she had prepared a beautifully decorated *stupa chedi* to enshrine the three great royals, and on the left and right were *stupa* for their attendants, large enough to fill the earth and to reach for the city in the skies above.[171] For his part, his majesty King Phichaiphitsanukon did likewise. They exchanged many messages of affectionate tone and announced a royal stipulation specifying the day for the interment of the ashes. Each in their own territory, the two great rulers conducted ceremonies of the most lavish kind, each of supreme magnificence. A great almsgiving took place throughout the land, and all the people without exception joined in a wondrous merit making. (656)

Every lord, every noble, and every commoner,
and every man and woman in all the land,
made merit for the benefit of their king
and with great fidelity commended him to the heavens.[172] (657)

It is a glory to the lips to recite this tale,
like a heavenly garland, carefully made,
an adornment for the ear on every occasion,
like a sachet that, only lightly touched, gives strength to the heart. (658)

It is completed as the great king composed it,
praising the dignity of Phra Lo, a genuine man, and
his brave attendants, who preceded their king in death,
the finest in this world and surpassing all the heavens. (659)

It is completed as the noble king[173] set it down,
this tale in verse of Phra Lo, surpassing man.
Whoever listens to it is sure to be entranced and will not tire of
     hearing
of the power of first love, of lovers genuinely and truly in love. (660)

ENDNOTES

Introduction

1. H. H. Prince Bidyalankarana, a man of letters as well as a gifted poet, presented this view quite clearly in a 1926 lecture for the Siam Society, which published his thoughts in its journal later that year. In "The Pastime of Rhyme-Making and Singing in Rural Siam," 101–127.

2. Such criticism began in the 1950s and was often echoed during the period of student unrest of 1973–76. See Chetana Nagavajara, "Literary Historiography and Socio-Cultural Transformation: The Case of Thailand," 71.

3. Perhaps the more telling question would be the ongoing value to modern Thai scholarship of a canon that was both established and, in effect, closed by royal fiat more than a hundred years ago.

4. Chanthit Krasaesin, *Prachum wannakhadi Thai phak 2 Phra Lo Lilit*, 4–6. Chanthit says that he compiled his text from twenty-five manuscript volumes, which he dates to the time of the third reign (1851–68), and while he identifies each source by the name of its then owner, no additional details are included. In an appendix to his work he lists thirty-seven volumes, saying that they are held by the National Library and identifying them by both owner's name and library number. Unfortunately, that identifying information does not coincide with the information that is given for the various volumes currently held in the collection, which includes fifty-four volumes. The library uses a numbering system of its own creation, one that seems to have been changed over time, and it includes only the name of the

individual or institution from which it obtained each volume and the date of the acquisition. The library has also grouped most of the volumes by content so that all the volumes that include the beginning portion of the tale are stacked and numbered together; next are volumes that contain a second portion, and so on. Again unfortunately, except for those that include the beginning of the tale, the volumes all begin and end at different points, so the library groupings do not facilitate text analysis, and it does not seem possible to be certain which ones might have once made up a complete text. There are indications that as many as four complete texts may have been separated in this cataloging effort. One complete rendition (numbered 46a, 46b, and 46c) has inexplicably been spared this separation and been left intact. A fourth volume is numbered 46d, but rather than being part of the single full text, it appears to be a gathering together of fragments of the text—apparently remnants of damaged volumes that were at some point bound together.

5. His bias toward modern forms is not without precedent. See Chetana, "Literary Historiography," regarding Prince Damrong Rachanuphap and his views of textual studies. See also Bidyalankarana, "The Pastime of Rhyme-Making and Singing in Rural Siam," for that author's views on the necessity of modern education for success in the poetic arts, as well as what he saw as the comparative weakness of those he referred to rather dismissively as unlettered "rhymesters" of earlier periods in history.

6. Pluang, *History of Thai Literature,* 145–53. Although entitled a history, the book is at least as much an anthology, and includes lengthy excerpts of a number of texts chosen by the compiler. It was first published in the 1960s under the title *Prawat wannakhadi Thai samrap nak sueksa,* (History of Thai literature for students).

7. Cholada, *An Lilit Phra Lo chabap wikhro lae thot khwam,* 537–38.

8. Sumonnachat, "Sop suan rueang kan taeng Phra Lo," 79–83. The dual pronoun system is clearly the source of a great deal of confusion in the text, with great variation in both the manuscript volumes and modern interpretations. By far the greatest confusion surrounds the third person dual form *kha* (ขา) (rising tone) "they two," which is often mistaken for *kha* (falling tone) (ข้า) "slave, servant."

9. See Wipha Senanan Kongananda, *Phra Lo: A Portrait of the Hero as a Tragic Lover*.

10. For a full treatment of this point see Bickner, *An Introduction to the Thai Poem "Lilit Phra Law" (The Story of King Law)*.

11. The phonetic similarity between these Thai and English terms is purely coincidental.

12. J. Marvin Brown is generally credited with having coined the term. In his dissertation and several related articles he has speculated at length about the many aspects of the changes that brought about modern speech forms.

13. In the terminology of comparative linguistics, the three categories are generally referred to as A, B, and C, respectively. The three categories encompassed all syllables ending in a continuant sound—that is, one in which the vocal cords are vibrating.

14. Some details of modern tone pronunciations appear to be clues to the contrasts that might have distinguished the ancient categories. For example, the glottal constriction that is found in the pronunciation of some words might be a holdover from the ancient system. Compare the word "to look for" *ha* (หา), pronounced with rising tone, and the word "five" *ha* (ห้า), pronounced with falling tone, or the words "ghost" *phi* (ผี), with rising tone, and "older sibling" *phi* (พี่) with falling tone. The second word of each pair must be pronounced with increasing glottal constriction, sometimes called "creaky voice," if it is to satisfy the ear of a critical Thai speaker, whereas the first in each pair may not exhibit such constriction. It is possible that this glottal constriction is a holdover from one of the ancient tone categories. Also suggestive is the similarity in most dialects of the southern branch of the Thai family between the tone contours associated with the modern first tone (*ek*) category and those associated with checked, or "dead," syllables with a long vowel, suggesting some phonetic similarity.

15. For the sake of simplicity, I omit discussion of syllables with an unvoiced final consonant, known in linguistic terminology as "checked" or "closed" syllables,

and in Thai terminology as *khamtay* (คำตาย) or "dead" syllables. For the complete picture see Bickner, *An Introduction*.

16. Sunthon Phu lived during the second and third reigns of the Bangkok era. The sound play that he creates in his work is astonishingly complex, so complex that it defies attempts at quantification or analytical representation. His mastery was so thorough that he left little for subsequent poets to explore, and it has been said that he exhausted the creative possibilities of the *klon* form. A solution of sorts has been the addition of arbitrary requirements, such as specifying the initial sound at the beginning of each line of the stanza. The practice of distinguishing stanza types according to such small variations may have originated with Indic forms, which when borrowed directly are known as *chan* (ฉันท์) and when borrowed through the intermediary of Khmer language texts are known as *kap* (กาพย์). This sort of categorization mimics the technique that was used to create the original source forms, which are made up of intricate rhythmic patterns that have no real correlation in Thai, and it has thus hindered study of *Lilit Phra Lo* by leading attention in inconsequential directions. A thorough examination of the variations found in the manuscript volumes suggests strongly that ancient poets who told the tale did not indulge in such minor tweaking of their forms. It appears instead that modern scholars, familiar with the borrowed forms and the techniques used to identify them, have applied those techniques in an anachronistic manner to earlier, indigenous forms and have mistaken ancient spellings or manuscript errors for purposeful manipulation. There is variation in the text stanzas that is worthy of further study, but that cannot be undertaken effectively until the limitations imposed by the weaknesses of the printed editions are fully resolved.

17. The misunderstanding really begins with viewing the text through the lens of literacy rather than orality. The ancient poets worked in oral forms, and literacy was not a factor. The text as we know it is not the same as a modern work (one that is quite literally a written one) but is a written approximation of an oral work. Over the course of time some words that appear in that record came to have spellings that no longer accurately reflect their original pronunciations. The most commonly

encountered of such words are now spelled with the first tone mark but appear in the text in positions in which a word with the second tone is expected. One example is the verb *len* (falling tone) "to play," which is written in modern Thai as though it originated in the *ek* category (spelled เล่น), but actually belongs historically in the *tho* category (spelled เหล้น). Such words are said to be instances of "erroneous second tone" (*tho thot* โทโทษ) spellings, or somewhat less judgmentally, "required second tone" (*tho bangkhap* โทบังคับ) spellings. In fact, though, the spelling found in the text is the historically accurate one.

18. For a thorough treatment see Bickner, *An Introduction*.

19. The expression appears only in the first stanza of the text as we know it today in what is labeled here as the invocation. It does not appear to be contemporaneous with the original tale. Nonetheless, the meaning change discussed here suggests that it is was appended to the text long ago.

20. The use of the doublet is so common in contemporary colloquial Thai that its presence or absence is all but a defining feature of skillful spoken discourse. Adult learners of Thai have a very difficult time mastering the skill, in the same way that adult Thai learners of English have a difficult time moving from the formal register of speech that is taught in classroom work into the informal, colloquial register.

21. Thomas John Hudak discusses the role of reduplication in modern speech and poetic forms in *The Indigenization of Pali Meters in Thai Poetry*. See especially chapter 2, "The Aesthetics of Sound, 25–44.

22. I have borrowed the label "invocation" for these passages from Nidhi, *Pen & Sail: Literature and History in Early Bangkok*, 32.

23. Prakhong Nimanhaemin, in "Sapphanam thawiphot nai phasa Thai boran" (Dual pronouns in ancient Thai), posits a fourth form in the paradigm: *ra* (รา) "we two" (inclusive), that is, speaker and addressee, with the implication that *rao* should be seen as "we two" (exclusive), that is, speaker and another, but not addressee. The word *ra* does appear in the text, most often at the end of a line of *khlong si*, where it may represent an aside to the audience. But that position does not allow for interpretation based on context, so the question awaits further study.

24. Yet another type is distinguished in textbooks, and that is called *khlong sam* (*sam* meaning "three"), with the name again indicating the number of full hemistichs in the stanza. But such a stanza is actually just the shortest possible stanza of *rai*, and there are no structural or poetic differences that justify categorizing them differently from longer stanzas of *rai*. Labeling them *khlong* actually serves only to obscure the difference between the two—*rai*, which has no elaboration following the full hemistich, and *khlong*, which does. The first hemistich of such a stanza is linked to the next (in the manner typical of *rai*) by a rhyme from the last syllable to an early syllable in the next stanza, and it is not embellished as are hemistichs of either of the other *khlong* forms. It is more in keeping with the overall pattern to consider such stanzas as *rai* rather than as *khlong* and to dispense with the term *khlong sam* entirely.

25. A further distinction is made between types of *rai* and *khlong* based on the ending pattern used in a given stanza, especially the final hemistich. A stanza that ends in a four-syllable hemistich, with the expected tone sequence in the first two syllables, is known as *suphap* (สุภาพ) "well formed," as opposed to one that ends in a shorter hemistich of only two syllables, which is known as *dan* (ดั้น) "to push." Still another distinction is made for *rai* stanzas that have neither ending pattern and simply stop after a full hemistich. Such a stanza is called *rai boran* (ร่ายโบราณ) "ancient *rai*," and is regarded as the least sophisticated type. In fact, only a handful of the 660 stanzas in the text have the shorter *dan* ending pattern, and only one stanza of *rai* has no discernable ending pattern. Still, much has been made of these differences as supposed evidence of development of the verse forms from simple toward more complex. These differences are actually minimal, at most, however, and the common assumption that the poetic forms found in Phra Lo are examples of a developmental process from simplicity toward complexity, or from less polished forms toward more accomplished forms, is tenuous at best. The assertion is really part of an unjustified bias toward modern forms that needlessly denigrates both the oldest Thai narrative text and the skills of those who developed it. The far more

likely and more satisfying explanation for these few examples in the text is simply that the extant manuscript copies are corrupt.

26. This pattern of inter-stanza rhyme has either been overlooked or misunderstood in modern analysis. See Bickner, *An Introduction*, for a full treatment.

27. All of the dialects of the family underwent such changes and must have done so at roughly the same time. The details differ somewhat from one region to another, but the general pattern of change remains the same.

28. For a summary of such accounts, see Klaus Wenk, "Thai Literature as reflected in Western Reporting during the 17th to the 19th Centuries."

29. It is more useful to think of *khlong* and *rai* in descriptive terms rather than in terms of rules. The forms grew out of the rhythms and features of what was then the ordinary speech of the day, without need for self-conscious rule creation, as was no doubt the case with the original *klon* forms following the systemic sound changes that brought about modern speech. It is possible that the propensity for rule-based conceptions of poetry so common in modern scholarship arose along with attempts to create poetry using patterns borrowed from Indic languages. Those languages employ vastly different phonological and syntactic patterns from those of Thai, and the use of most of those forms requires significant distortion of Thai pronunciations. (See, for example, Bidyalankarana's *Phra Non Kham Chan* in which the author uses no fewer than twelve different *chan* patterns in his retelling of the story of King Nala. Many of those passages require pronunciations that would render the them unintelligible if they were presented only orally and without a written text.) Efforts to maintain the creative possibilities of *klon* in the wake of the master poet Sunthon Phu most likely also helped generate the concept of poetry based on arbitrary rules.

30. Nidhi's contention that *khlong* and *rai* "were not used in the literature of the ordinary people" but were used in court literature of early Ayutthaya (Nidhi, *Pen and Sail*, 7–8) is not supported by current knowledge of language development.

31. These references to Parry's insights are based on the three articles in the references list.

32. For further details see Bickner, "Some Textual Evidence on the Tai Sounds *ai and *au."

33. A. L. Becker, "The Journey Through the Night: Some Reflections on Burmese Traditional Theater," 156.

34. The utilitarian nature of a "plot book" would also explain why the manuscript volumes are not decorated in any way; they were meant to be used, not admired.

35. Jacques Brunet ("The Comic Element in the Khmer Shadow Theater," 27) speaks of "interludes" in Khmer shadow theater performance, separate from the main story, and intended "to provide relaxation for the spectators, and for the dancers. The characters employed are little [sic] peasants who speak a local idiom and make the spectators laugh with their puns, ambiguous words and onomatopoeia." Such comic figures are, of course, staples in Thai popular entertainment to the present day.

36. A. L. Becker, "The Journey Through the Night: Some Reflections on Burmese Traditional Theater," 154–64, speaks of the great importance of theater throughout Southeast Asia. Speaking specifically of Burma, then the main focus of his research, he says it is one of two institutions by which people make sense of their lives, the other being Buddhism. That characterization would seem to apply equally well to Thailand of the time. Typically, he says, "this theater is outdoor, commonly performed all night on a temporary stage, and accompanied by a mainly percussive orchestra." Such performances can still be seen in modern day Indonesia.

37. Chua Sariman, "Traditional Dance Drama in Thailand," traces the Thai shadow theater to the Srivijaya Empire, citing a note in the Palatine Law of King Borommatrailokanat in 1458.

38. See Bidayalankarana ("The Pastime of Rhyme-Making and Singing in Rural Siam") for a charming and revealing account of elaborate verbal contests based on skill in extemporaneous composition. They attracted large numbers of participants and were played out on the waters in and around Ayutthaya at the time. The contest that the prince observed seems to have been an example of one type of what Terry Miller and Jarenchai Chonpairot ("A History of Siamese Music Reconstructed from

Western Documents, 1505–1932," 123) call "repartee," specifically a "boat song" known as long ago as 1688. The prince's account is a small window onto rural life and is revealing as an example of the distance in both attitude and awareness between an elite urban intellectual and the bulk of the speech community.

39. In her thesis "Laughter for Spirits, a Vow Fulfilled: The Comic Performance of Thailand's Lakhon Chatri Dance-drama," anthropologist Mary L. Grow found a still-vibrant popular tradition of *lakhon chatri* performance in southern Thailand long after common wisdom thought of all such traditions in Thailand as moribund, if not entirely lost. The form's ongoing popularity had apparently been overlooked in academic circles.

40. See Hartmann, "Computations on a Tai Dam Origin Myth," for one example. The wording used in that tale as Hartmann found it, not in written form but in the memory of senior speakers of the dialect, clearly shows its roots in a three-tone system.

41. See James Chamberlain, "*Thao Hung* or *Cheuang*: A Tai Epic Poem" regarding the Lao language epic *Thao Hung ru Cuang*, which also shows evidence that its verse forms developed from a three-tone system. That text includes a figure known as Thaen Lo. M. C. Chand Cirayu Rajani speaks of a "Caw Sam Lo" in the literature of the Shan kingdom of modern Myanmar, whom he equates with Phra Lo, Thaen Lo, and with the figure "Khun Lo" from the chronicles of the Lan Chang kingdom in modern Laos (cited in Phaitun Phrommawichitra, "Chak Lilit Phra Lo thueng Chao Sam Lo nai wannakam Thai Yai").

42. Clifford Geertz, *Negara: The Theatre State in Nineteenth-Century Bali*, 13. The whole monograph is devoted to this idea of the theater state.

43. Such associations later became a staple of the poetic lament known as *nirat* (นิราศ), composed in *klon* form and depicting the loneliness experienced by travelers separated from home and loved ones.

44. Striving for perfection is important to both royal families. Note that Lady Bunluea, Phra Lo's mother, has urged him to rule as a perfect king, and that the princesses are similarly urged on by their grandmother, who in stanza 476, for

example, reminds them to seek to perfect themselves in each of the four movements, saying, "reclining, sitting, standing, and walking—perfect each of them equally."

45. See especially Joseph Campbell, *The Hero with a Thousand Faces*.

46. This idea is developed in *The Masks of God: Primitive Mythology*, the first volume of Campbell's four-volume work.

47. Discussed in an interview with Bill Moyers, transcribed in Joseph Campbell, *The Power of Myth*, 105.

48. I began my work with the edition of 1975, the most recent one available to me at the time. Over the ensuing years, I have compared that edition with a number of subsequent printings and can find no substantive changes either to the text or to the accompanying glossary. Occasional typographical errors have appeared in some printings only to be corrected, albeit without comment, in subsequent years. But other than such apparently inadvertent changes, the text seems not to have been altered.

49. See, for example, the attempts by M. R. Seni Pramoj in his *Interpretative Translations of Thai Poets*, among others. Whatever a reader may feel about the outcome of that author's efforts it seems clear that attempts extending beyond a stanza or two could not be sustained.

50. The most forceful voice is that of M. C. Chand Chirayu Rajani, who argues for translating poetry as poetry. I acknowledge his position and his reasoning but most respectfully disagree.

51. Milman Parry and his students also noted that in the ancient oral compositions they studied, the poetic unit nearly always coincides with the syntactic unit. So consistent is this finding that they used it as one of the tests to determine whether or not a given text is a reasonably faithful written record of oral improvisation. See Ivan Illich and Barry Sanders, *ABC: The Alphabetization of the Popular Mind*.

52. This was an enormous and tedious job that I could never have accomplished without a great deal of help. Dr. Em-on Chitasophon, then chair of the Department of Thai at Chiang Mai University, graciously provided working space and helped recruit participants for a compilation of all the versions of every passage found in

the manuscript copies of the text. It took about six weeks to complete, and the students worked at it each day outside of class and when their other responsibilities allowed. Their enthusiasm and good humor made the time pass quickly, and their attention to accuracy and to detail resulted in an exceptionally valuable tool.

Lilit Phra Lo

53. Chanthit Krasaesin (*Prachum wannakhadi Thai*, 2) interprets the term *Lao Kao* (ลาวกาว) as a reference either to the people of Luang Prabang, the old royal capital of Laos, or to residents of the northeastern part of modern Thailand, presumably with ethnic connections to Luang Prabang. Phra Worawet, though, (*Khu mue Lilit Phra Lo*, 1) says that it is a reference to the city of Vientiane, which is the administrative capital of modern Laos. Cholada Ruengruglikit (*An Lilit Phra Lo*, 79) refers to speculation from Dr. Prasert Na Nagara that agrees with those quoted above, but adds the possibility that the term is a reference to residents of the Thai provinces of Phrae and Nan. Charles F. Keyes ("Hegemony and Resistance in Northeastern Thailand," 156) associates the Lao Kao with Lan Chang or Luang Prabang in Laos. The significant point in all of this is the rivalry between, on the one hand, those in the central plain—evidently the "Thai" in this passage—and on the other those of the northern and northeastern parts of modern Thailand and Laos. It is important to note that the rivalry as presented in this stanza does not include speakers from other language families who play significant roles in the early history of the region, neither the Khmer to the east nor the Burman to the west. This political rivalry within the Thai-speaking domain (or "Tai," to use the spelling introduced by French scholars who first came to know the language family in areas where the dental stop is not aspirated), which is of great significance in the development of the modern political landscape of the area, does not appear in any form in the story itself. It is not clear whether those rivalries arose after the tale came into being or whether they simply were not a concern to those responsible for the original creation of the tale. In either case, though, from a thematic perspective the content of the five verses that make up what is here labeled "invocation" do not

appear to be contemporaneous with the tale itself. Considering also that they are both structurally and thematically distinct from the forms used in the rest of the text it seems highly likely that they are a later addition. See Bickner, *An Introduction*, for further details regarding structural differences. Regarding content see also Nidhi, *Pen and Sail*, 24) regarding the changing content of such invocations, which would suggest that this one dates from the early part of the Bangkok era.

54. The expression used here is *phaephai* (แพ้พ่าย). In modern Thai usage the word *phae* means "to lose," but in all other dialects of the language family it means the opposite, "to win." See the introduction for further comment on the significance of this meaning change.

55. The nine gems, according to Chanthit (*Prachum wannakhadi Thai*, 4) are diamond, ruby, emerald, topaz, garnet, sapphire, moonstone, zircon, and lapis lazuli.

56. Phra Worawetphisit (*Khu mue Lilit Phra Lo*, 1) identifies the first four stanzas of the text as we know it today as an introductory passage. These stanzas are similar to the ceremonial paying of respect to one's teachers that often precedes a performance in modern Thailand and that is found at the beginning of many older literary texts. Phra Worawet is the only commentator to separate these stanzas from the rest of the text, and it is unfortunate that others have not taken note. Both thematic and structural factors set these stanzas apart from the rest of the text, suggesting that they were added at some point following the creation of the original story.

The structural differences help to identify the stanzas as a later addition, but the implications of the thematic differences have not yet been addressed. The first stanza is noteworthy because it is partly an inventory of sorts of politically ambitious Thai-speaking polities, described in decidedly bellicose terms as having fallen to the dominant one, Ayutthaya. The second stanza is a paean to the unnamed ruler of that city, who is praised for his power and military prowess, and also for the wealth that followed from his successes. The passage is not out of keeping with other texts of the time and of later days, but it is completely out of keeping with the rest of the poem, in which such tensions are not even mentioned. The battles that do take place in the story of Phra Lo are never associated with ethnic rivalries.

57. The king's name is composed of *maen* (แมน), meaning "god" or "angel," and *suang* (สวง), meaning "heaven" or "divinity." The queen's name is likewise composed of two words, both still in common use: *bun* (บุญ), meaning "virtue; merit," and *luea* (เหลือ), which means "to exceed." The king's name clearly attributes to him an origin beyond the mundane world, and that of the queen suggests that she is suffused with the highest of qualities.

58. The extant manuscript copies of the text are inconsistent here, with some placing the city to the east and others to the west. The original wording, if such a concept can even be used with a story derived from an oral tradition, has long been lost, along with any certainty of what the east–west orientation might have signified to an ancient storyteller and why it might have been important enough to insert at this point in the tale, where it is thematically unrelated to the subject matter that precedes it.

59. The tale of Phra Lo actually begins at this point. The opening hemistich, *klaw thung khun phu hao* (กล่าวถึงขุนผู้ท้าว), is a ringing assertion that the tale to come will be filled with characters and events of an epic scale. The opening is as arresting and memorable as Virgil's dramatic opening of *The Aeneid*: "I sing of arms and of the man" (*Arma virumque cano*).

60. The name "Phimphisakhonrat" is a combination of three nouns meaning "mark," "ocean," and "king," respectively. Campbell (*The Power of Myth*, 257) refers to a figure in the Mahabharata, a "Universal Monarch named Ocean (*sagara*)," that uses the same word. Thus the name suggests something like "bearing the mark of [king] ocean."

61. The name Phichaiphitsanukon is composed of three nouns meaning "victory," "Vishnu," and "arm," respectively. Darawadi is composed of two elements, the noun *dara* meaning "star," plus *wadi*, defined as a feminine ending. The 1999 dictionary of the Royal Institute (p. 1052) cites this passage as its example of this

usage. All the names would be difficult to render in English, but the suggestions of divine power and grandeur are clear.

62. Students of Thai will recognize the princesses' names as two frequently encountered words that translate into English as "friend" (*phuean*) and "expensive; costly" (*phaeng*). The two words appear only as names in the story and one may wonder if they were not less frequently used in earlier times. A more poetic rendering, which might better parallel ancient usage, would be "beloved" and "precious."

63. The significance of these names is difficult to assess. Among the many meanings found in various dictionaries for *ruen* (รื่น) are "joyful; fresh; comfortable." Meanings given for *roy* (โรย) include "wither; weaken; wilt; sprinkle." The two characters have little individuality in the poem as it exists today, so we have no internal evidence that might indicate the significance of the names. If the modern meanings correctly reflect ancient usage, though, it could be that the names were intended to evoke a conceptual paradigm or a ritual activity of some sort that would have been familiar to the audience, or that was somehow important to the original conception of the story, but that has since passed from memory.

64. This lady's family connections and home city are not mentioned. Her name has two components: *laksana* (ลักษณ) meaning "quality; type", and *wadi* (วดี) a female combining form meaning "to have," thus suggesting "epitome of womankind," "admirable lady," or the like.

65. The three realms are the lower world, the world of humanity, and the heavens. The lower world is the dwelling place of demons and the location of hell. Titans, demigods and gods reside in the heavens.

66. The comparison is to the fruit known as *maprang* (*Bouea macrophylla*, known variously as the Marian plum, gandaria, and mango plum). The comparison seems to be based on the smooth texture of the ripened fruit.

67. In explaining similar words, dictionaries of Sanskrit refer to a pointed hook by which the god of love incites or inflames lovers. Phra Worawetphisit (*Khu mue Lilit Phra* Lo, 14) offers a similar interpretation, likening the hook to an elephant goad. Students of Western literature may recognize a similarity with Cupid's arrow.

68. The description calls to mind statues, carvings, and paintings from various locations in the region, in which the representation of the neck includes concentric curved lines.

69. The term used here is *ngam* (งาม), which in modern Thai means "beautiful; lovely." While it is frequently used with women, it is seldom applied to men. These ten stanzas and others with similar content suggest that concepts of beauty, or at least the scope of the terms used for such concepts, have changed significantly over time.

70. The expression suggests the image of a vine with no tree upon which to cling. The vine motif appears often in the text.

71. Note the power of the spoken word as presented in these passages and elsewhere in the story. Listeners are overwhelmed by the descriptions, and Phra Lo will likewise be smitten when descriptions of the two princesses reach him.

72. The word that appears at this point in the published editions of the text is the noun *kha* (ข้า) (falling tone), with the modern Thai meaning of "servant." One of the manuscript copies, however, omits the tone mark, giving *kha* (ขา) (rising tone), the now largely forgotten third-person dual pronoun meaning "they two." There are thus two possible readings for the opening of the stanza, which is spoken in the voice of the narrator, "the servants," on the one hand, and "the two of them," on the other. The emphasis on status that is present in the first wording is not present in the second, and that emphasis seems out of keeping with the feeling that the ladies-in-waiting are trying to express. It is interesting to note that three of the manuscript copies have at this point *phuea,* the first-person dual pronoun, taking the passage out of the narrator's voice and giving it to the ladies-in-waiting as "we (two)," suggesting that there was uncertainty about how to present the passage to an audience. See the introduction for more on this issue.

73. In this stanza, the princesses Phuean and Phaeng reply to a query posed by their ladies-in-waiting, Ruen and Roy. It is by far the best-known stanza of the poem, having been selected for notice as early as the first known Thai treatise on poetry, the *Chindamani*, thought to have originated in the mid-1700s, which gives

this stanza as its example of the *khlong* verse form (Department of Fine Arts, *Chindamani lem 1–2*, 32). Today, nearly all Thai speakers who have completed high school literature courses have memorized it and recall it even years later. At first glance, it is puzzling that this stanza is the only one that is given such attention; its content is of only minimal significance for the development of the plot, and it includes no particularly clever wording or interesting imagery. No explanation is ever attempted for the attention lavished on this one stanza above all others, but it is likely due to the fact that it is the only one of the nearly three hundred *khlong si* stanzas in the poem that happens to meet exactly the structural requirements prescribed by scholars. All other stanzas fail in some way to comply with the idealized form as presented in textbooks. The variations are sometimes significant, such as a seemingly misplaced rhyme link, and are sometimes quite minor, such as a seemingly extra syllable, but analyses that see these variations as flaws are unwittingly more attuned to the visual aspects of a written record of the poem than to the auditory aspects of a verbal presentation. The variation again suggests that the ancient poets were not creating a unique text that they expected be read but were instead working in an oral form, repeatedly recreating and developing a spoken text that they expected to be heard. They were, moreover, working with a language that was fundamentally different from the speech of the present day. For a detailed treatment of such issues of orthographic considerations versus auditory ones, see Bickner, *An Introduction*.

74. The expression used in this passage and repeated throughout the text is *somsu* (สมสู่). The term as it is used in contemporary speech still means "to unite" and while it has clear sexual implications, the somewhat negative connotation of modern usage seems not to be present in the text.

75. See stanza 11, in which Phra Lo is also described with a rain motif. In that stanza he is likened to an incarnation of the Hindu god Indra, and here Phra Phuean and Phra Phaeng are likened to the attendants of Indra. The passages foreshadow the so-called "miracle" passages (stanza 537ff), in which the three will join in what is presented as a coupling of divinities.

76. The passage foreshadows the magic images that the powerful Samingphrai will create later in the poem (stanzas 117 and 131) in his magic charms.

77. Chanthit (*Prachum wannakhadi Thai*, 66) says that this pose is a standard indication of suffering. The passage that he chooses to support his assertion, however, is from the *Ramakian*, the Thai version of the Rama story that is attributed the reign of Rama I, written centuries after the text of *Phra Lo* came into being.

78. In reference to this passage, both Phra Worawet (*Khu mue Lilit Phra Lo*, 30), and Chanthit (*Prachum wannakhadi Thai*, 31) state that one who aspires to rule as king must acquire eighteen types of knowledge. Neither scholar, however, provides specifics.

79. The text becomes disjointed at this point, and the structure of this hemistich does not fit the expected pattern of five stressed syllables, broken into two phrases of unequal length with no rhyme linking the phrases. Instead, the wording *pu mo thao chao mo luang* (ปู่หมอเฒ่าเจ้าหมอหลวง) is made up of an equal number of stressed syllables, broken into two phrases of three syllables each and linked by rhyme, does fit the expected pattern of the modern *klon* form of poetry, a form that did not exist at the time the tale came into being. Furthermore, the rhyme link, consisting of the fourth and fifth syllables of the hemistich, is between syllables from two different tone categories. The modern spoken system allows for such a rhyme, while the ancient spoken system apparently did not. Thus, the wording in the hemistich as we have it today is modern, so there has been either an insertion or perhaps a rephrasing of older material.

80. The manuscript volumes vary noticeably in this stanza, and for the first line the Ministry of Education text compounds the problem by choosing the wording found in only one of the eighteen manuscript copies that have this stanza. Significantly, that volume is labeled number 10, and it includes at its beginning a statement indicating that it was the personal property of King Rama V, a fact that no doubt accounts for its wording being chosen for the printed edition even though it does not agree with any other manuscript copy. While reverence for the king and his possessions is understandable, such ahistorical choices, both here and elsewhere

in the text, hinder scholarly research. Ironically, Chanthit notes the wording from volume 10 but dismisses it as illogical. The manuscript wording (สองศรีเฉลียวฉลาด เกี้ยว กลชิด) is the basis for my translation of this stanza.

81. The concept of soul calling, or *riak khwan* (เรียกขวัญ), is a familiar one in modern Thailand and is often associated with folk Buddhist practice, although no such association is suggested in the text. It is considered efficacious when, for example, an illness or a catastrophic turn of events has brought an individual to a state of great emotional agitation or distress. That individual is said to have experienced a loss or scattering of the soul, a condition known as *khwan hai* (ขวัญหาย).

82. This act of transformation foreshadows the more complex transformations that Samingphrai will perform in stanzas 77 and 78.

83. The reference is to the god Vishnu, who in the Hindu tradition carries qualities that are similar to those of Cupid in Western traditions.

84. This stanza includes the first of the many nature catalogs, in which the poets provide a variety of compilations of plants, flowers, trees, fish, birds, and animals in the surroundings. Sound play, in the form of alliteration and rhyme, is an integral part of the catalogs, which grow increasingly complex.

85. The manuscript versions of this passage differ. Of nineteen volumes that have this passage, eighteen are legible at this point, and of those, ten use the word *mu* "pig; boar" (หมู) suggesting the translation given here. Eight copies use the term *mu* "group; herd" (หมู่), which would perhaps suggest "herd(s) of bears." The words differ only in the presence or absence of the tone mark, and in this case consultation with the manuscripts cannot resolve the ambiguity. Since bears are normally solitary creatures, however, the translation favors the first wording.

86. Interpretations differ regarding the number of animals seen by Ruen and Roy. The wording does not make the number specific, and some commentators see a single animal, while others see two. The women are approaching a powerful spiritual entity, one that, as later passages make clear, demands respect for his attainments. If the feline presence functions as do portal guards, long a common motif in the art and architecture of the region, then there would be a pair of animals,

which is the interpretation followed here. In either case, the transformation that is depicted prefigures that which Samingphrai is about to make in his own appearance. These changes and those he performs on the entirety of the forest clearly demonstrate that Samingphrai possesses mastery over all aspects of the natural world.

87. *Choen* (เชิญ) "to invite" is still used with august beings and objects in modern Thai. In preparation for a procession in which a Buddha image is to be moved, for example, the image is said to be "invited" to participate.

88. The Royal Institute Dictionary (p. 268) defines the term as a "name for a type of bird" but then cites this passage as an example.

89. The term used here is *lamang* (ละมั่ง), a bow-antlered deer. The female is *la-ong* (ละอง) or simply *ong* (อง). Interestingly, Chinese also has separate names for the two genders of this deer (James R. Chamberlain, personal communication).

90. The expression rendered here as "waterfowl" is *nokhok* (นกหก), which in modern usage denotes birds in general. At this point in the text, however, the subject matter of a lengthy catalog shifts from land-dwelling birds to waterfowl. Perhaps the modern Thai term for waterfowl, *nokpetnam* (นกเป็ดน้ำ), had not yet come into use.

91. The *chakphrak* (จากพราก), the fourth of the terms in this part of the catalog, is identified by the Royal Institute Dictionary (p. 303) as a type of waterfowl, with the added information that in literature it carries the implication of separated mates who call out for each other in the night. It is, of course, impossible to know whether it was the name, a compound of two verbs, "to depart," and "to be separated," or the literary application of that name that came first.

92. This is the first fully elaborated nature catalog in the poem. See the introduction for more information.

93. The expression used here is *chua fa lom kan* (ชั่วฟ้าล่มกัลป์), "until the sky collapses (at the end of) the kalpa." The 1999 Royal Institute Dictionary defines a kalpa as the span of time from the creation of the world by the Hindu god Brahma until its consumption in a final conflagration sent by Siva to destroy all. This period

is known as a "Brahma day" and includes one thousand great eras or 4.34 billion human years.

94. Washing the hair is a major part of love charms, and this passage may be a reference to such magic (Chris Baker, personal communication).

95. Chanthit (*Prachum wannakhadi Thai*, 141) says this device is created from several types of bamboo fiber woven together to form a ball-like object. He likens it to a sort of tumbleweed that when caught by a sea breeze bounds quickly along a beach.

96. Unlike the attendants to the princesses, who are specifically introduced in the text, the attendants to Phra Lo simply appear here. They are called Kaew (แก้ว) "crystal; glass" and Khwan (ขวัญ) "spirit; heart."

97. The word used here is *thet* (เทศ), from the Indic *desh*, used in modern Thai as a combining form suggesting foreign origin as in *makhueathet*, meaning "tomato" and formed by combining *makhuea* "eggplant" with *thet*, suggesting that it was once seen as an unfamiliar variety of a local plant. The form is also used in country names suggesting "place of," as in *bangalathet* (บังกลาเทศ) "Bangladesh," although such a term is more likely a fairly recent borrowing than a Thai coinage. Chanthit (*Prachum wannakhadi Thai*, 152) cites the presence of this word in the text as evidence that it came into being only after contact with foreign countries had been established, apparently assuming isolation to have been the norm, but a single word is slight evidence for such a conclusion.

98. There has been speculation about the appearance of this flag, at least some of which is based on a purported variation in the manuscripts between the word *chai* (ไชย) "victory," with a short vowel, and the word *chai* (ชาย) "side; edge," with a long vowel. The manuscript volumes give no grounds for such speculation, however; all have the word for "victory."

99. See stanza 5 and its brief statement on the relative locations of Suang and Song, a statement that is rendered inconsistently in the manuscripts. The wording of this stanza, at least, is consistent within the manuscripts; it seems to suggest that

Song lies to the east and Suang to the west, although any possible significance of that juxtaposition is not specified in the text.

100. Chanthit (*Prachum wannakhadi Thai*, 165) says that it was once the custom that a queen would not reveal herself and would speak only from behind a curtain. That Bunluea chooses to open the curtain, he suggests, indicates the importance that she places on these consultations. The conceptual separation created by the curtain seems also to reflect concepts of the *devaraja,* or god-king of Hindu mythology.

101. The practitioner's name is Sitthichai (สิทธิชัย). The Royal Institute Dictionary (p. 1193) defines his name as denoting skill in magic arts. No source for the term is cited, but many other entries in the dictionary are attributed to the Phra Lo story and that may be the case here, as well..

102. Phra Worawet (*Khu mue Lilit Phra Lo,* 79) explains that such a celebration required a *baisi* (บายศรี), a ritual object arranged in tiers, with the number of tiers determined by the status of the subject of the offering. The tiers were filled with various foods, and at the peak was a cone filled with rice, with shelled boiled rice affixed to it. Notables and relatives sat around the *baisi,* holding lighted candles and wafting the smoke toward the person for whom the ceremony was being conducted, who was seated next to the *baisi.* In modern usage, the term refers both to the ceremony and to the central object, the inverted cone of rice, which is said to represent a sacred mountain and is colorfully decorated, typically with flowers and strips of cloth, and surrounded with boiled eggs and other foods associated with good fortune. Today, the *baisi* ceremony seems to be associated more with Lao custom than with Thai, but it also has counterparts in other cultures of both mainland and insular Southeast Asia. The concept of the sacred mountain is important in both Hindu and Buddhist cosmology.

103. The passage calls to mind tantric themes, in which each of the gods has a specific animal as its accustomed vehicle (personal communication, Patrick Lanahan).

104. The *sala hoen* (สลาเหิน) is an enchanted concoction of betel that will travel to a desired location and hide itself in the victim's betel tray. When the concoction is then consumed, the victim will be smitten with love. Betel chewing, although largely abandoned in modern Thailand, is well known as once having been an important feature of both interpersonal and ritual behavior throughout Southeast Asia, and magic of the sort found in this text is found elsewhere as well. See Guillermo (*Epic Tales of The Philippines*, 1), for instance, for a folk tale from the Philippines in which "the betrothal ceremony was arranged by the magic betel." The Ministry of Education text (*Nangsue an kawiphon rueang Lilit Phra Lo*, 185) offers an additional detail, saying that the betel will, when taken in by the victim, become a carpenter bee and induce rapturous love. The bee appears again in stanzas 333 and 523.

105. The stanza numbered 148 in the Ministry of Education edition is not to be found in any of the extant manuscript copies. The translation for this stanza is included here for the sake of completeness, and so as not to disturb the numbering system created for that edition, but it is certainly a modern insertion and should be considered as such in studies of the text. Curiously, the Ministry text includes a footnote giving a purported variant reading for this non-existent stanza, indicating incorrectly that it is to be found in "some copies" of the manuscripts. Chanthit (*Prachum wannakhadi Thai*, 185), however, notes that the stanza is absent from all the manuscripts that he studied, and he speculates that it is a rewording, presumably of stanza 149, but without suggesting when that rewording might have been done.

106. Ten months is the traditional Thai reckoning of the normal human gestation period.

107. There are many differences in this stanza between the printed versions and the extant manuscript copies, and a thorough comparison clarifies many spots of uncertainty. One example will be useful at this point to illustrate a major problem with published editions of the poem. The second hemistich of this stanza as it appears in the ministry text reads *chonni nat rat ranthot* (ชนนีนาฏราชรันทด) "the queen moaned." This wording is comprised of six syllables, divided into phonetically equal segments that are linked by the rhyme formed by the middle two syllables.

The student of Thai poetry will recognize in this passage a pattern characteristic of the *klon* (กลอน) form of poetry that has developed out of the five-tone system of modern Thai. As much in keeping with modern tastes as this pattern may be, however, it is strikingly unlike the rest of the text, in which a hemistich is nearly always composed of five stressed syllables, divided into two phrases of unequal length, and in which rhyme within a hemistich is so rare that it appears to have been purposely avoided. Of the twelve manuscript copies that are legible at this point, only four use the wording that appears in the published editions, while the other eight do not include the word *nat* (นาฏ). Instead they read *chonni raat ranthot* (ชนนี ราชรันทด), which gives the same meaning, but this wording conforms with the expected *khlong* pattern. The word in question is an honorific, used today in royal titles, and it adds nothing to the sense of the passage. It seems likely that it was a modern insertion, perhaps intended as an improvement upon the passage by making it align more with modern concepts of elegant speech. Such aberrant passages are scattered throughout the story and when taken together suggest that the editing of the manuscript for publication was guided by a bias toward contemporary norms. While some of the problematic wording does indeed exist in the manuscript copies, in nearly every case in which there was a choice between two or more wordings, the published editions opt for the wording that more closely approximates modern forms. This bias is exhibited repeatedly in Chanthit's study. He is at pains to list as many variants as he was able to find, but nearly always states a preference for the one phrased in a more modern pattern, frequently offering the justification that his choice "sounds better."

108. Chanthit (*Prachum wannakhadi Thai*, 250–51) and Phra Worawet (*Khu mue Lilit Phra Lo*, 109–10) both attempt to divide the text to define the seven attributes referred to by Queen Bunluea, but their divisions do not agree with each other. Chanthit goes so far as to present this stanza divided into seven numbered sections, each intended to be one of the attributes. There is, however, no support for this sort of division in the manuscript copies, which include no numbering and no orthographic clues with which to delineate the seven attributes. Phra Worawet, on

the other hand, presents his divisions in a footnote, saying that he has divided the material along thematic lines, but he admits that he could accept a different arrangement. The divisions suggested by each of these scholars are indicated below with numbers in brackets. Those of Phra Worawet are marked with numbers in standard font, those of Chanthit with numbers in italic font.

And then the beautiful queen mother moaned, her heart a melancholy void. "Peerless Lord Law, I love you more than my eyes or body, more than my life or my existence. Now you are to leave me, forsaking your mother, forsaking your royal city. A great ruler has seven attributes, that you must remember. Memorize these words of your mother and do not abandon them. Do not neglect the rites of the noble born. [1] Do not be negligent, forgetting yourself. [1] Do not associate with untruthful people. Consider carefully and only then act. Weigh each word and only then speak. Do not bring difficulty onto your subjects. Judge all matters of state straightforwardly. [2] Govern your kingdom so that all will have comfort. Eliminate all distress both internal and external. [2] Concern yourself with every department. Do not be attracted to falsehood. Deliberate, and then follow the way of justice. [3] What you would prevent, prevent completely. What you would suppress, suppress artfully. [3, 4] Examine both your guides and your servants. Select only the trustworthy. Choose your counselors with care. Instill boldness in your people. Destroy the parasites who would weaken your realm. [4] Punish subjects who violate our laws. Deter those who dare to aid our enemies. Suppress wickedness so it cannot arise. [5, 5] Do not seek ripeness before its time. [6] Do not tether a horse from both sides. Do not drag poison behind you. Do not cause people to hate and secretly curse you. [7] Conduct yourself so that others will love you. [6] Persuade others to seek after the heavens. In the future, the divinities will praise you, so you must do what is right. Do not neglect contemplation. [7] Be unhurried in your deliberations so that your dignity will not be lost. When the skies and the earth and the heavens come to their end, may the consuming conflagration not destroy you. Follow these instructions of your mother. Oh, your mother's greatest love, may you prosper."

Chanthit speculates that the actual number of attributes might actually have been twenty-seven, beginning with the admonition, "Do not be negligent, forgetting yourself," and ending with "Persuade others to seek after the heavens." The error, he says, must have been in copying old sayings with which to create the passage and inadvertently specifying the incorrect number. He also asserts (*Prachum wannakhadi Thai*, 245) that the material in the stanza predates the rest of the poem, speculating that much of it is composed of aphorisms that were common at the time and were included by the poets who created the story as we know it today. He further states that the language of the passage is very ancient, and that the aphorisms contained in it are comparable in age to the sayings of Phra Ruang of Sukhothai. He does not, unfortunately, offer support for these speculations, discuss specific examples, or cite other texts as sources from which the sayings may have been taken. These assertions are reminiscent of the reactions of western students of Shakespeare who upon first encountering *The Tragical History of Hamlet, Prince of Denmark*, criticize the author for supposedly including hackneyed sayings in his passages, not realizing that the play is, in fact, the source of those now very familiar expressions.

109. Chanthit (*Prachum wannakhadi*, p. xcix) feels that this stanza is a later insertion, along with stanzas 200, 208–9, 217–18, and 257. He attributes them to Somdet Phra Maha Sommanachao Krom Phra Paramanuchitchinorot, premier poet of the third reign of the present dynasty and author of *Lilit Talengphai*, "The Defeat of the Mon." Without citing specific examples, he offers as evidence what he says are modern phrasing and wording similarities between these stanzas and those from the more recent work. He reasons that these stanzas must have been inserted between 1843 and 1849, the period during which Rama III ordered the collection of information on a variety of topics, which was made available in the form of engraved tablets that are displayed throughout Wat Phra Chetuphon (Wat Pho),

where they can still be seen today. Phra Paramanuchitchinorot was responsible for the creation of tablets dealing with the poetic arts. The extant manuscript copies in the National Library collection do not offer evidence either to support or to call into question Chanthit's assertion. The copies that include this portion of the poem all include these stanzas, and there is as much variation in those copies as there is for other sections of the text. Determining comparative age for the copies does not seem possible. It appears that there must have been a decision at some point to remove any identifying notation from the manuscript copies and to replace it with a standardized label of the library's own creation, which includes very limited information. The only manuscript copy (number 8) to still include its original labeling gives the year of its creation as 1860, well after the period that Chanthit is referring to.

110. Phra Worawet (*Khu mue Lilit Phra Lo*, 115) identifies the four groups as infantry, elephant troops, cavalry, and vehicle troops.

111. Phra Worawet (*Khu mue Lilit Phra Lo*, 118) notes that there is no rhyme link between the final syllable of stanza 214 and an early syllable of stanza 215, concluding that something has been omitted. The comment is a peculiar one, since there generally is no rhyme link between a stanza of *khlong song* and a subsequent stanza of *khlong si*, and the absence of such a link here, rather than being exceptional, is characteristic of the text. For a full treatment of how intra-stanza rhyme links function in the poem, see Bickner, *An Introduction*, especially chapter 7, pp. 207–218.

112. The Ministry of Education edition includes this stanza in a footnote, saying that it appears at this point "in some [manuscript] copies." In fact, the stanza appears in twelve of fifteen copies that include this portion of the story. Other stanzas in different portions of the story are omitted from various manuscript copies but are not treated as suspect in the ministry text. Chanthit notes that the stanza was omitted from the version published in 1926, which seems to be the only justification for questioning its validity.

113. The translation given here is based on wording that is included in the Ministry of Education text as a footnoted alternative reading. Of the fifteen extant

manuscripts that include this passage, however, twelve have that "alternative" wording and only three have the main reading. Chanthit (*Prachum wannakhadi Thai*, 265) also favors the ministry's alternative wording but professes skepticism about it and several other stanzas (see note 57 above). In Chanthit's work this stanza is identified as 173a and the next as 173b, which is a departure from his normal numbering pattern.

114. This stanza is included in the ministry text only in a footnote saying that it appears in some manuscripts. In fact, of the fifteen copies that include this portion of the story, only three do not have this stanza. I have numbered it 218b to avoid disrupting the numbering of stanzas established by the ministry text.

115. The description calls to mind some scenes of traditional Indonesian, or perhaps more correctly Javanese, dance that depict the behavior of Arjuna, hero of the Mahabharata, in which graceful manipulation of the sash is an important motif.

116. The *mangkorn* (มังกร) is a dragon-like creature that appears frequently in temple art in Southeast Asia. It is often depicted at the base of stairways and doorways, with the great serpent, or *naga*, issuing from its mouth. The Royal Institute Dictionary (p. 450) identifies it as a figure from Chinese mythology, without mention of the motifs of South Asia.

117. The name of the elephant is made up of elements denoting victory and power, elevated with a royal prefix.

118. While the word "Sindhu" in Modern Thai has come to mean horses in general, there is no way to know if that more general meaning had developed by the time this text was formulated. The sense here seems to parallel the Western perception of the Arabian horse as the epitome of grace and speed.

119. The titles and ranks used here and elsewhere throughout the text are echoed in more recent times in royal appointments and in contemporary times in military and police ranks. The text does not focus on such issues, so there is some potential ambiguity. The status and responsibilities associated with each title and with each numerical designation do not play a part in the events of the poem, and so it is not possible to interpret those details based on this text.

120. The published editions of the poem have *phan* (พัน) "one thousand" in this passage, but the manuscripts all have (พล) "troops; forces."

121. In Indic mythology, the half-giant, half-eagle *garuda* serves as the vehicle of Vishnu.

122. The break between stanzas 229 and 230 in all published editions of the poem is not to be found in any of the manuscript volumes. Instead, the material forms a single lengthy stanza.

123. This passage and subsequent ones appear to be forerunners of the modern *nirat* (นิราศ) poem, in which a traveler expresses grief over separation from his loved one, who is brought to mind by what he encounters during his travels.

124. The image of a rabbit is the traditional Thai interpretation of the patterns of light and dark on the surface of the moon.

125. See Robert Bickner, "Reflections On a Literary Dispute Between Jit Phumisak and Phra Worawetphisit," for details on the heated disagreement that broke out between Phra Worawetphisit, longtime teacher of literature at Chulalongkorn University, and his then student and later widely recognized intellectual and dissident, Jit Phumisak. The disagreement was over the pronunciation and meaning of the name for this condiment, which Jit recognized as a borrowing from Khmer. He evidently corrected Phra Worawet's interpretation of the word, earning his teacher's undying resentment in the process.

126. The line is based on wordplay involving the name of a type of tree and the verb "to mix together; to pet." The following verses are built on similar wordplay involving nouns and verbs in their normal usage and homophones of those words used as flower and tree names.

127. The words *ket* (เกด), a kind of fruit tree, and *ket* (เกศ, spelled เกษ in the manuscripts) "hair," are homophones, both pronounced in modern speech with the low tone.

128. The term translated here as "shawl" is *sabai* (สไบ), which refers to a cloth worn over one shoulder and fastened at the opposite waist and that is sometimes

defined as a "breast cloth." Modern versions can be very elaborate or quite simple, depending on the setting in which they are to be worn.

129. This catalog consists of parings of birds and trees with names that are fully or partly homophonous. The phrasing makes clear which is the bird name and which is the tree. Only a few of the names have English equivalents.

130. This catalog pairs the Thai word *ka* (ก) "crow" with five different partly homophonous tree names.

131. The wordplay here is with the phrase *chang nao* (ช้างน้าว), which is both a plant name and a phrase meaning "elephants bend."

132. This catalog is constructed with the names of three mammals—the tiger (*suea*), the deer (*kwang*), and the elephant (*chang*)—and homophonous tree names.

133. This stanza, which combines alliteration and rhyme, is a catalog composed of words for types of monkeys, their offspring, their manner of moving, and their eating habits. A transcription provides at least a taste of the stanza as we know it today.

> *Lang ling ling lot mai lang ling*
> *Lae luk ling long ching luk mai*
> *Ling lom lai lom thing ling lot ni na*
> *Lae luk ling lang lai lot liao lang ling*

134. This stanza includes more than forty tree and plant names, most of which have no common English counterpart, all arranged in hemistichs grouped primarily by alliteration. Dictionaries and botanical resources do not always correspond, suggesting variation in naming conventions, perhaps by location or time. An additional consideration is that dictionaries, including that of the Royal Institute, often give definitions based on a word's appearance in this text, making for the possibility of circularity in the assigning of meanings. In any case, the passage is certainly intended as a poetic tour de force, and its significance derives from the poetic skill with which it is arranged, not from a taxonomic exactness. Criticisms that an item in a given catalog is not grouped appropriately in scientific terms simply miss this point. The phonetic transcription gives the reader who does not

control Thai orthography a sense of the intricate sound play that makes this stanza so notable. However, the modern pronunciations give only an approximation of the ancient phonology, in which the array of syllable-initial consonants was much more complex than it is today.

135. The stanza numbered 267 in the Ministry of Education text is not found in any of the extant manuscript copies. It must be considered a modern insertion that does not predate the first use of print technology. It is included here because the stanza has become part of the modern text that Thai readers expect to see included.

136. This passage, *chop bat thuli than sai klao* (จบบาทธุลีธาร ใส่เกล้า), amounts to a verbal obeisance, akin to modern pronominal forms in which a speaker addresses only the dust beneath the foot of the monarch, suggesting that the speaker is not worthy even to refer directly to any more elevated aspect of the royal presence. The corresponding first-person form refers to the top of the head of the speaker, the implication being that no other portion of the speaker's body is fit to be mentioned. The same motif, in more or less elaborate phrasing depending on the situation, is used elsewhere in the poem. See, for example, the depiction of Phra Lo taking leave of his mother and then his wife in stanzas 194–96, 204, and 219.

137. This passage is difficult to interpret. The wording of the published editions includes the verb *phuk* (ผูก) "to tie up," and perhaps suggesting "to assign." However, that word does not appear in any of the manuscript copies, where the noun combining form *phu* (ผู้) "person" is to be found instead. The Ministry of Education text acknowledges the historically correct reading but refers to it as an alternative reading.

138. Phra Worawet (*Khu mue Lilit Phra Lo*, 179) says that these colors are red, white, purple, yellow, and blue. Chanthit (*Prachum wannakhadi Thai*, 404) cites black, red, green, white, and yellow. Other sources cite a slightly different selection of colors.

139. The term used here is *hamsa*, or *hong* (หงส์), meaning "goose" or "swan." In Indic mythology, it is a vehicle of Brahma, among other associations.

140. The term is an epithet for Shiva, and thus appears to be a reference to India.

141. The sound play in the stanza is based on the word *ket* (เกศ) "hair," and a homophonous flower name.

142. The final line of the stanza is an elaborate alliteration spread over two hemistichs, the first of five syllables and the second of four: *khla khu khlueng khla khlao khoi khlao khlo samon* (คล้าคู่คลึงคล้าเคล้า ค่อยเคล้าคลอสมร).

143. The five desires are form (*rup*), taste (*rot*), scent (*klin*), sound (*siang*), and touch (*samphat*). In modern usage, the expression has clear sexual implications.

144. The fish mentioned here is the *chon* (ช่อน) or "snakehead murrel." According to Wit Tiengburanathum (*Photchananukrom Thai-Angkrit*, 384) the term is also used as a reference to the penis.

145. The term "thousand streams" is the name of a vessel used to sprinkle water during Thai coronation ceremonies and is royal vocabulary for bathing (Royal Institute Dictionary, p. 1146). Chris Baker suggests that the term may derive its meaning as a reference to Indra, who is said to have one thousand eyes (personal communication).

146. This stanza does not appear in the edition of the poem published by the Ministry of Education, but it does appear in eleven of thirteen extant manuscript copies and so should be considered a part of the text. The stanza is numbered 411a here to preserve the numbering of the Ministry of Education edition. See also the note for the following stanza.

147. The Ministry of Education text wording does not specify the color of the lotus here, although twelve of thirteen extant manuscript volumes refer to a red lotus, a reading that is given in a footnote. It appears that stanza 411a and 412 were merged at some point.

148. This stanza is not in any of the extant manuscript copies; it must be a modern insertion.

149. Stanzas 511 and 512 clearly illustrate how elusive the text can be. The précis of Tamra Na Muangtai (*Phra Lo*, 114) states that the stanzas are very difficult to translate, and that the author is not sure of his interpretation. Chanthit (*Prachum*

wannakhadi Thai, 609), on the other hand, says that these stanzas are clear and not in need of interpretation.

150. In modern times a watch is generally defined as a period of three hours.

151. The word used here is *atsachan* (อัศจรรย์) "miraculous; wondrous," and it has become the designation for metaphorical depictions of sexual activity in the phrase *bot atsachan* "miracle passages."

152. Twelve of the thirteen manuscript volumes that have this passage are legible at this point, and all end the first hemistich with *mai* (ไม้) "tree."

153. The expression used here is *chaoku* (เจ้ากู), which combines *chao* "lord" with the ancient first-person pronoun *ku*; it does not appear elsewhere in the poem. The reader will recognize the pronoun from the famous Ramkhamhaeng inscription, often cited as the first appearance of writing in Thai. Clearly the coarseness associated with the pronoun in modern urban usage was not present at an earlier time. Chanthit (*Prachum wannakhadi Thai*, 635) glosses the expression as a pronominal reference to Phra Lo, equating it with *chaokhongku* (เจ้าของกู), which includes the noun *khong* in its familiar modern usage as a possessive marker.

154. The word that ends the hemistich in the printed editions is *suai* (สรวย), spelled as though it were a borrowing from Khmer, but unknown in contemporary Thai. Chanthit (*Prachum wannakhadi Thai*, 635) glosses the word as *suai* (สวย) "pretty," evidently believing it to have been a purposeful misspelling of that word invented by the poets to conform to the expected tone placement pattern. Điêu Chính Nhim and Jean Donaldson (*Ngũ-vựng Thái-Việt-Anh*) however, note a White Thai cognate word meaning "oval," hence the translation given here. The word must have fallen out of use in Thai only fairly recently. Of the thirteen manuscript copies that include this passage, eleven have what would have been the modern Thai form for "oval" (สว้ย), suggesting that those who made the manuscript copies during the middle of the nineteenth century recognized the word, but those who set the story in type not many decades thereafter did not. One copy has "pretty" (สวย) and one has the royal vocabulary word *sawoei* (เสวย) "to eat"; the spelling found in the printed editions is not to be found in any of the manuscripts. The "sr" consonant

cluster is not to be found in words of Thai origin, but it does appear frequently in Khmer words, many of which have been borrowed into Thai. That the printed editions came to have the spelling that they do appears to be an instance of hypercorrection employing Khmer conventions.

155. The word used here is *nat* (นาด), which the Royal Institute Dictionary (p. 576) defines as "to extend the arms in a beautifully graceful manner," perhaps reminiscent of classical dance postures, which reflect the degree of refinement of each character.

156. Chanthit (*Prachum wannakhadi Thai*, 663) describes the preparation of such powders: "The ingredients consist of sandalwood, fragrant wood resins, the civet extract, and saffron. The pith of the sandalwood and the fragrant resin must be powdered and then mixed with sandalwood oil, and then dried into a powder. For use it must be dissolved with water or in sandalwood oil." See also the endnote for stanza 611.

157. In contemporary times, when the trunk of the banana tree is to be used for fodder, it is cut into thin slices across the width of the trunk.

158. The term used here is *krachae chung chamot* (กระแจะจุงชะมด). Chanthit (*Prachum wannakhadi Thai*, 696) describes this powder as "a fragrance based on the substance produced by the testes of the civet (a striped, four-footed animal with a long face, a pointed snout, and a long tail) which it deposits by rubbing on the bars [of its cage]. It is collected on a betel leaf and heated until it releases a fragrant smell. It can then be mixed with various cosmetics." Chanthit also gives detailed directions for preparing the substance.

159. The story of Phra Lo as we know it today is often said to be a Buddhist text, but with only this single reference to Buddhist practice, which could easily be a more modern insertion, that characterization seems at best to be overly simplistic.

160. Literally, "the breast of the kingdom seemed about to overturn."

161. A more literal translation would be "It is beautiful to see them standing in death."

162. There is no mention in the text of an act of conferring titles upon the attendants. This is another of the unresolved details that combine to suggest that the text is from an oral tradition.

163. *Meru* (เมรุ) is the name of the sacred mountain that stands at the center of the Hindu universe. In modern times the term is also used to refer to the funeral pyre and the elaborate wooden tower structure that is built for public cremations of individuals of high rank.

164. While the general sense of this passage is clear, the published Thai explications of the poem offer differing interpretations of what a *butsabok* (บุษบก) would have looked like and how it might have been used. While it is clear that decorations were elaborate, it is not clear how they might have been arranged, or exactly what they might have looked like.

165. The published texts use the word *chamniam* (จำเนียม), which the Royal Institute Dictionary defines as "to know one's station; to act according to one's station." This passage of *Lilit Phra Lo* is then cited as the source, along with the assertion that the word is derived from *chiam* (เจียม), with the same meaning. In fact, however, none of the extant manuscript volumes has this word. All thirteen of the volumes that have this passage have instead the word *thamniam* (ทำเนียม), described as an archaic equivalent of *thiam* (เทียม) "to make the same as, or similar to the real thing." McFarland's definition for this word is "to be untrue, feign, pretend"—hence the choice of "lifelike" for this translation. Part of the confusion here may stem from the repetition of the latter word in the next two hemistichs.

166. The *khotchasi* (คชสีห์)—*khot*- (คช-) "elephant" and *si* (สีห์) "lion"—is a mythological beast with a lion's body and an elephant's trunk and can be seen in modern times as the emblem of the Thai Ministry of Defense. *Garuda*, a figure derived from Indic mythology, and in Thai known as *khrut* (ครุฑ), is a formidable bird-like being and is considered the vehicle of Vishnu. It has long been used as a royal insignia, and in 1911 King Rama VI adopted it as the emblem of the nation. The *naga* (นาค) is a serpent, sometimes thought of as a divinity and often depicted with seven heads. In Hindu mythology the *naga* has several roles, including serving

as a resting platform for Vishnu, and as a rope used in churning the cosmic sea of milk at the creation of the world. In Buddhist mythology the *naga* is said to have aided the Buddha during his final meditation, lifting him above rushing flood waters by coiling its body beneath him, and sheltering him from the falling rain by spreading its hood above him.

167. Note that the twelve extant manuscript copies that include this passage do not support the published editions. Instead of *singha* (สิงห์) "lion," they have *singkha*, (สิงค์ and other spellings) "highest point" or "mountaintop."

168. This reference to a memorized message is a tantalizing detail, perhaps a reflection of the relative importance of the time attached to the spoken word as opposed to writing. Recall also the great power of both spoken and sung descriptions of Phra Lo on the princess sisters, and of the sisters on Phra Lo, in turn, that appear earlier in the story.

169. Note that the emissaries are sent to Bunluea, the mother of Phra Lo, and not to Laksanawadi, his wife and queen.

170. The expression used here is "108 cities." This number is used in modern expressions to indicate a number beyond counting; it seems to have that same meaning here.

171. Thai Buddhist temple compounds typically include what Westerners recognize as a stupa, a stylized mountain and representation of the cosmos. The terms *stupa* and *chedi* are both used in modern Thai speech to refer to such structures, although *chedi* is the far more common of the two. Unfortunately the text does not include any suggestion of how the terms might have been used in the past, or of how a *stupa chedi* might have differed from a *chedi*.

172. The translation here is based on the reading given as an alternate (สวามิภักดิ์ ถ้วนหน้า ชื่นหน้าชมสวรรค์) in the Ministry of Education edition, which actually is the reading of eleven of the thirteen manuscript volumes that include this passage.

173. Printed editions of the text use a term for "prince" at this point, but that wording is spurious. All of the manuscript volumes have a term that means "king." See the introduction for details.

BIBLIOGRAPHY

Becker, A. L. "The Journey Through the Night: Some Reflections on Burmese Traditional Theater." In Osman, *Traditional Drama*, 154–64.

Bickner, Robert J. *An Introduction to the Thai Poem "Lilit Phra Law" (The Story of King Law)*. Monograph Series on Southeast Asia. DeKalb: Center for Southeast Asian Studies, Northern Illinois University, 1991.

——. "Some Textual Evidence on the Tai Sounds **ai* and **au*." In *Papers on Tai Languages, Linguistics, and Literatures In Honor of William J. Gedney on his 77th Birthday*, edited by Carol J. Compton and John F. Hartmann, 223–30. DeKalb: Center for Southeast Asian Studies, Northern Illinois University, 1992.

——. "Reflections On a Literary Dispute Between Jit Phumisak and Phra Worawetphisit." In *Papers from the Tenth Annual Meeting of the Southeast Asian Linguistics Society*, edited by Marlys Macken, 87–96. Tempe, AZ: Program for Southeast Asian Studies, Arizona State University, 2002.

Bidyalankarana, H. H. Prince. "The Pastime of Rhyme-Making and Singing in Rural Siam." *Journal of the Siam Society* 20, no. 2 (1926), 101–27.

——. *Phra non kham chan*. Bangkok: Salakinbaeng Ratthaban, 1955.

Bloom, Harold, ed. *Homer* (Modern Critical Views). New York: Chelsea House Publishers, 1986.

Brunet, Jacques. "Themes and Motifs of the Cambodian Ramayana in the Shadow Theater." In Osman, *Traditional Drama*, 3–4.

Brunet, Jacques. "The Comic Element in the Khmer Shadow Theater." In Osman, *Traditional Drama*, 27–29.

Campbell, Joseph. *The Masks of God: Oriental Mythology*. New York: Penguin Press, 1991. First published 1962 by Viking Press.

—————. *The Hero with a Thousand Faces*. 2nd ed. Princeton: Princeton/ Bollingen, 1968. First published 1949 by Princeton University Press.

—————. *The Power of Myth with Bill Moyers*. New York: Doubleday, 1988.

Chamberlain, James. "*Thao Hung* or *Cheuang*: A Tai Epic Poem." *Mon-Khmer Studies* 18–19 (1990): 14–34.

Chand Chirayu Rajani, M. C. "On Translating Thai Poetry." *Journal of the Siam Society* 67, no. 1 (1977): 293–357.

Chanthit Krasaesin. *Prachum wannakhadi Thai phak 2 Phra Lo Lilit*. [Thai literature collection part 2 Lilit Phra Lo]. Bangkok: Thai Wattana Panich, 1954.

Chetana Nagavajara. "Literary Historiography and Socio-Cultural Transformation: The Case of Thailand." *Journal of the Siam Society* 73, parts 1 & 2 (January & July 1985): 60–76.

Cholada Ruengruglikit. *An Lilit Phra Lo chabap wikhro lae thot khwam* [Reading Lilit Phra Law: Analysis and interpretation]. 2nd ed. Bangkok: Chulalongkorn University Press, 2010.

De Campos, Joaquim. "Early Portuguese Accounts of Thailand." *Journal of the Siam Society* 32, no. 1 (1940): 1–27.

Department of Fine Arts, Thailand. *Chindamani lem 1–2 banthuek rueang Chindamani lae Chindamani chabap Somdet Phra Chao Borommakot*. [Chindamani books 1–2 the Chindamani and the Chindamani of King Borommakot]. Bangkok: Bannakhan, 1971.

Department of Fine Arts, Thailand, *Lilit Phra Lo: chabap hosamut heang chat* [Lilit Phra Lo: Edition of the National Library]. 11th printing. Bangkok, 1968.

Điêu Chính Nhim and Jean Donaldson. *Ngữ-vựng Thái-Việt-Anh* [Tai-Vietnamese-English vocabulary]. Saigon: Bộ Giáo-Dục Xuât Bản, 1970.

Eck, Diana L. *Darsan: Seeing the Divine Image in India.* New York: Columbia University Press, 1998.

Geertz, Clifford. *Negara: The Theatre State in Nineteenth-Century Bali.* Princeton: Princeton University Press, 1980.

Grow, Mary Louise. "Laughter for Spirits, a Vow Fulfilled: The Comic Performance of Thailand's Lakhon Chatri Dance-drama." PhD diss., University of Wisconsin, 1991.

Guillermo, Artemio R., ed. *Epic Tales of the Philippines: Tribal Lores of Filipinos.* Lanham, MD: University Press of America, 2003.

Hartmann, John F. "Computations on a Tai Dam Origin Myth." *Anthropological Linguistics* 23, no. 5 (1981): 183–202.

Hudak, Thomas John. *The Indigenization of Pali Meters in Thai Poetry.* Monographs in International Studies, Southeast Asia Series, No. 87. Athens, OH: Ohio University, 1990.

Illich, Ivan, and Barry Sanders. *ABC: The Alphabetization of the Popular Mind.* San Francisco: Northpoint Press, 1988.

Keyes, Charles F. "Hegemony and Resistance in Northeastern Thailand." In *Regions and National Integration in Thailand 1892–1992*, edited by Volker Grabowsky, 154–82. Wiesbaden: Harrassowitz Verlag, 1995.

McFarland, George Bradley. *Thai-English Dictionary.* California: Stanford University Press, 1944.

Miller, Terry E., and Jarenchai Chonpairot. "A History of Siamese Music Reconstructed from Western Documents, 1505–1932." *Crossroads: An Interdisciplinary Journal of Southeast Asian Studies* 8, no. 2 (1994): 1–163.

Ministry of Education of Thailand. *Nangsue an kawiphon rueang Lilit Phra Lo* [Reading edition of the poetic composition Lilit Phra Lo]. Bangkok: Khuru Sapha, 1975.

Nidhi Eoseewong. *Pen & Sail: Literature and History in Early Bangkok.* Edited by Chris Baker and Ben Anderson. Chiang Mai: Silkworm Books, 2005.

Niyada Laosunthon. "Lilit Phra Law: Historical Study." Unpublished paper presented at a conference entitled "New Dimensions in Literary Criticism and Literary Studies." Silpakorn University, Bangkok, January 19, 1989.

Osman, Mohd. Taib, ed. *Traditional Drama and Music of Southeast Asia*. Kuala Lumpur: Dewan Bahasa dan Pustaka, 1974.

Parry, Milman. "The Traditional Epithet in Homer." In Bloom, *Homer*, 11–18.

——. "The Traditional Metaphor in Homer." In Bloom, *Homer*, 25–31.

——. "The Traditional Poetic Language of Oral Poetry." In Bloom, *Homer*, 19–24.

Phaitun Phrommawichitra. "Chak Lilit Phra Lo thueng Chao Sam Lo nai wannakam Thai Yai" [From Lilit Phra Lo to Chao Sam Lo in Shan literature]. *Krungthep Thurakit*, August 3, 1997.

Pluang Na Nakhorn. *Prawat wannakhadi Thai* [History of Thai literature]. Bangkok: Thai Wattana Panich, 2002.

Prakhong Nimanhaemin. "Sapphanam thawiphot nai phasa Thai boran." ["Dual Pronouns in Ancient Thai"]. *Phasa lae Nangsue* 18 (1976): 91–98.

Prem Burachatra, Prince. "Magic Lotus: A Romantic Fantasy; an Adaptation for the English Stage of the Fifteenth Century Siamese Classic Pra Law," 1946. An adaptation of the author's *Magic Lotus: A Romantic Fantasy*, Chatra Books, 1937.

Reynolds, Craig J. *Thai Radical Discourse: The Real Face of Thai Feudalism Today*. Studies on Southeast Asia No. 3. Ithaca: Cornell Southeast Asia Program, 1987.

Royal Institute Thailand. *Photchananukrom chabap ratchabandit sathan 2542* [Dictionary of the Royal Institute 1999]. Bangkok: Nanmeebooks, 2003.

Sariman, Chua. "Traditional Dance Drama in Thailand." In Osman, *Traditional Drama*, 165–71.

Seni Pramoj, M. R. *Interpretative Translations of Thai Poets*. Bangkok: Thai Wattana Panich, 1968.

Sumonnachat Sawatdikun, M. R. "Sop suan rueang kan taeng Phra Lo" [Investigation into the composition of Phra Lo]. *Warasan khong samakhom khon wicha haeng prathet Thai* [Proceedings of the Society for Scholarly Study of Thailand] 3 (1945): 1–54.

Tamra Na Muangtai. *Phra Lo.* Bangkok: Thai Wattana Phanich, 1996.

Wenk, Klaus. "Thai Literature as reflected in Western Reporting during the 17th to the 19th Centuries." *Journal of the Siam Society* 86, parts 1 and 2 (1991): 219–26.

Wipha Senanan Kongananda. *Phra Lo: A Portrait of the Hero as a Tragic Lover.* Nakhon Pathom: Faculty of Arts, Silpakorn University, 1982.

Wit Thiangburanadham. *Photchananukrom Thai-Angkrit* [Thai-English dictionary]. Bangkok: Ruam Sasn (1977) Ltd., 1992.

Worawetphisit, Phra. *Khu mue Lilit Phra Lo* [Handbook for Lilit Phra Lo] 3rd printing. Bangkok: Khuru Sapha, 1987.

Note on Dictionary Usage

Over the years I have consulted many dictionaries, and I am indebted to the authors thereof for their hard work and dedication. Because I have always been in the habit of cross-checking as many sources as possible, it would be difficult if not impossible to determine the source from which I first obtained a specific definition or piece of lexical insight. For this task of attempting to translate the wording of Phra Lo it is possible to point to three dictionaries that have been of the most assistance:

The *Royal Institute Dictionary* is generally regarded as the most definitive. I have always known it to be available in print, and its content went unchanged for many years and through many printings until the 1999 edition reached the market in 2003. That edition was expanded to include many modern entries, although as far as I can determine no attempt was made to expand on the original entries.

The late William J. Gedney, who spent many years in Thailand following the end of World War II, recalled that a decision had been made to include in the dictionary only information that all members of the drafting committee could agree upon. The result, he said, was that a great deal of potentially useful material was left out, especially with regard to the more obscure entries for which divergent opinions or variant usages might have been illuminating. This limitation is clear in a number of definitions that are based on what a given entry appears to mean in the Phra Lo text. For such entries the possibility of circular reasoning cannot be overlooked.

Dr. George Bradley's *Thai-English Dictionary* is very helpful for students of literature. His work began as a translation of the Royal Institute text, but he added to that a great deal of information on the Indic origins of individual words and their meanings in different contexts. He has also included botanical and taxonomic information regarding trees and plants, as well as the purposes for which material taken from them might have been used. While not of direct help in translating obscure passages, such information is very useful for developing a sense of the environment in which the story is located.

Finally, and at first blush perhaps inexplicably, I found very useful the dictionaries compiled by Wit Thiangburanatham. Several peculiarities and idiosyncrasies in his volumes suggest strongly that the author was not trained in lexicography or any related field, but despite his lack of technical expertise he must have had a deep and thoroughgoing interest in words. He seems to have been at pains to collect and include all the possible meanings for his entries, no matter how inconsistent they might have seemed. The result is often something of a jumble in which different levels of usage are not specified. For me, the great variation in his entries became an asset in attempting to sort through possible interpretations of obscure passages. That same variation, however, could easily be a hindrance to those who would use his work for less specialized purposes.